Favorite Days Out in Central Florida from 'The Villages' Residents

Gillian Birch

Copyright © 2012 Gillian Birch

All rights reserved. No part of this book may be reproduced, stored in a retrieval system or transmitted in any form or by any means without prior permission of the publisher, except by a reviewer who may quote brief passages in review to be printed in a newspaper, magazine, journal or on-line bookseller.

Cover Photo: De Leon Springs State Park

ISBN-10: 1481113054

ISBN-13: 978-1481113052

Dedicated to volunteers everywhere who enable our non-profit organizations to thrive, thanks to their generous contributions of time, talents, and love

CONTENTS

Preface	vii
1. Homosassa Springs Wildlife State Park	1
2. EARS – Endangered Animal Rescue Sanctuary	9
3. Marjorie Kinnan Rawlings Historic State Park	17
4. Ybor City Historic Walking Tour	24
5. Two Tails Ranch	31
6. Wild Bill's Airboat Tours	37
7. West Orange Trail	43
8. Forever Florida Swamp Buggy Coach Safari	51
9. Ringling Museum of Art & Mansion	57
10. Tarpon Springs	67
11. Silver Springs Nature Theme Park	73
12. St Augustine	81
13. De Leon Springs State Park	89
14. Daytona Beach	97
15. Don Garlits Museum of Dragsters & Classic Cars	103

PREFACE

When I asked residents of 'The Villages' to send me suggestions for their favorite days out, I could never have imagined the overwhelming response I would receive. I had no idea just how innovative, widely traveled, and fun-loving 'The Villages' residents are! The day trips that people submitted covered some fabulous places to visit, including state parks, animal sanctuaries, museums, gardens, stately homes, airboat rides, historic cities, and far more. Inevitably, many people suggested the same places, so generally I gave credit to the first person to come up with the attraction. Some used their own name; others preferred to use an alias. However, their personal comments make this a warm collection of days out, recommended by your friends and neighbors within 'The Villages' community.

Once I had my shortlist of new places to visit, I gamely set out to visit and photograph them all, and had a great time doing so. I "chuffed" with Bengal tigers, fed carrots to elephants, hung on for dear life on a thrilling airboat ride, marveled at the detailed model of a traveling circus at the Ringling Museum, explored the history and architecture of Ybor City, and was amazed at the fantastic Motor Museum that is right on our doorstep at the Don Garlits Museum of Drag Racing and Classic Cars.

I had a ball doing all these days out and I hope that as you dip into this book for ideas and inspiration, you will too. Follow in my footsteps and enjoy more hidden gems of Central Florida, along with the original day trips outlined in my first book, *Days Out in Central Florida from The Villages*. These books, together with my other published travel guides to Florida, are available in both paperback and ebook format, and they make great gifts for friends and neighbors. If you want to show off the natural beauty and diversity of Central Florida to visiting family and friends, then you only need to flip through the pages of these books to discover hot springs, walking trails, historic homes, botanical gardens, and sites of interest just a short drive away.

Dare I throw down the gauntlet again? I think so. If you can provide me with 15 more brilliant suggestions for days out, I will be happy to compile yet another book of *More Days Out in Central Florida from 'The Villages'* – it's up to you! In the meantime, enjoy all these wonderful trips as you explore this fascinating area with your family and friends.

Happy Trails!

WHAT'S WHAT

Suggested by: Each destination begins with a credit and short comment from the person who recommended the attraction. Some used their own name; others preferred to use an alias. Thanks to you all!

Introduction: A short description of the attraction and what it has to offer, to help you choose a day out that will best suit your needs.

Location: Full address, telephone number, and GPS co-ordinates to make getting there very easy. The official website address of the attraction is provided for more information.

Directions: The easy-to-follow directions and mileage to the destination all start from the **CVS Pharmacy on CR466 (GPS: 28.928, -82.016),** just in front of Publix Supermarket, so directions and mileage should be adjusted from that point.

Suggested directions follow quiet roads and scenic routes wherever possible, to make the journey as enjoyable as the actual attractions which are mostly less than an hour by car from 'The Villages'.

What to Do: This section gives a full and detailed description of what to expect and things to do at the attraction, including guided tours, personal tips, best times to visit, and other pertinent information for you to get the most from your visit.

Cost: Admission prices and cost of boat trips, guided tours etc. are all correct at time of going to press in late 2012. They are intended as a guideline only and may be subject to change in the future.

Open Times: For seasonal openings and annual events I have supplied general information and telephone numbers. It is advisable to call and confirm details before setting off.

Where to Eat: These are places that I have personally experienced or were recommended to me. The businesses did not know I was gathering information for a book; I was simply there as an ordinary paying customer.

Nearby: Once you have enjoyed visiting your chosen destination, other nearby attractions are suggested to extend your day out or to include as a detour on your journey home.

Favorite Days Out in Central Florida from 'The Villages' Residents

Favorite Days Out in Central Florida from 'The Villages' Residents

Homosassa Springs Wildlife State Park

Recommended by Linda, Village of Caroline who says:

"Homosassa Springs Wildlife Park used to be an old roadside attraction until the state of Florida bought it to protect the headwaters. They have manatee shows, snake shows, bear shows etc. There are just cyclone fences separating you from the alligators and when we took our grandsons, the five-year-old fell in love with them. Hope you enjoy it as much as I did"

The Ellie Schiller Homosassa Springs Wildlife State Park is one of the best ways to see rare and exotic Florida wildlife up-close and in beautiful surroundings along the shores of

the Homosassa River. Have you ever seen roseate spoonbills sifting the stream for food? Did you know that pink flamingoes were once common in southern Florida? And where else can you go down to an underwater observatory and see endangered West Indian manatees close up in clear spring waters that are teeming with fish?

Homosassa Springs Wildlife State Park is a 210-acre park with a host of activities all year round. The two recreational areas are linked by a boat trip, walking trail or trams which are all included in the entrance fee. The main entrance and Visitor Center with parking is located on US19 and includes a Manatee Education Center, gift shop, restrooms, and boat docks. Just ¾ miles away is the West Entrance to the state park on Fishbowl Drive. It has parking, the Wildside Café and the main wildlife attractions and boardwalk beside the Homosassa River.

Location

17 miles west of Inverness on US 19.

4150 South Suncoast Blvd
Homosassa, FL 34446
Tel: (352) 628-2311

GPS Coordinates: 28.801, -82.576

www.floridastateparks.org/homosassasprings/

Directions

Take US301 south to Wildwood.
Proceed west on CR44, through Inverness, until you reach Lecanto. Turn left here onto CR490. When you reach US19, turn south and the entrance to the park is on the right.

Distance from The Villages: 44 miles

Things to Do at Homosassa Springs Wildlife State Park

I would recommend parking at the main entrance on US 19 as the boat trip is so much fun as you are transported along the river to the main attractions. This entrance is also the place you will find complimentary kennels as dogs are not allowed into the state park.

After parking and purchasing your admission tickets, hop aboard the next tram or take the complimentary boat trip. The tram runs along the ¾ mile Pepper Creek Trail through some of Florida's most unspoiled natural habitat. It makes a very pleasant 15 minute amble for those who prefer to go at their own pace, and it is part of the Great Florida Birding Trail. However, the boat trip is a real treat. The pontoon boats sail gently along Pepper Creek taking about 20 minutes with an interesting commentary on the way out, and a quicker trip with no commentary on the return voyage.

Once in the wildlife park, plan your visit so you can participate in the three educational programs on offer which include a Manatee Program, Wildlife Encounters in the open-air auditorium and the Alligator and Hippopotamus Program. They are very interesting and well worth making a point of joining in – you are sure to learn something new from the expert Wildlife Care Volunteer Wardens and Park Rangers who present the programs and answer all your questions.

There is a 1.1 mile-long boardwalk that runs along both sides of the Homosassa River. It is lined with enclosures of native Florida creatures, many of which have been injured and need a permanent sanctuary home. The exception to the Florida wildlife is the 52-year old Nile Hippo nicknamed Lu, who can be seen basking on his own terrace or swimming in the pool. Be warned – do not stand behind him!

Prior to the creation of the Homosassa Springs Wildlife State Park in 1989, the area was a private attraction with various exotic animal exhibits. When it became a state park dedicated to preserving "The Real Florida", the non-native animals were moved to other permanent homes. This led to an outcry from local residents who had become attached to their very own hippo. Eventually Lu the hippo was given a reprieve and he was made an honorary Florida citizen to avoid deportation!

Before arriving at Homosassa Springs, Lu had been used in the filming of many TV shows and films including the popular *"Daktari"* series set in Africa. He quickly became a pampered attraction and was fed marshmallows tossed to him by visitors. Unfortunately this gave him a set of unhealthy yellow teeth which he is keen to show visitors when he opens his mouth wide for healthier treats of melon and bananas.

Weighing around 3,000 pounds or three tons, this giant lumbering creature moves in a seemingly ungainly manner on land but he swims gracefully in his pool with just his boggle eyes remaining above water. According to the very informative and humorous program presented by the volunteer warden, Lu puts away 15 pounds of hay and grain as well as plenty of fruit chunks every day. You can follow his thoughts on his very own Facebook page, Lu!

Opposite the hippo pool is the alligator lagoon with currently 11 resident alligators. Following the shady boardwalk along the river, the Wildlife Walk is a wonderful way to view many native animals including red wolves which are almost extinct in the wild, owls and birds of prey, a flock of pretty pink flamingoes, nesting pelicans and other birds. Being on the raised boardwalk, visitors are within close proximity of the wildlife, making it ideal for taking some stunning photographs.

The path leads through gates into the walk-in Shore Bird Aviary with a beautifully realistic seashore where the white sand is scattered with driftwood and an old boat. Visitors can purchase food to feed the unusual ducks, seabirds and herons in this excellent facility.

Walking further on around the clear spring-fed river, you will see sensitively designed naturalized enclosures with bears, river otters, panthers, bobcats, and a huge turkey displaying his black and white feathers to dramatic effect like a plump and disapproving Victorian lady. Take a short diversion to the Reptile House to see snakes and young alligators.

The Manatee Area is an enclosed section of the river which houses four West Indian manatees who can no longer survive without care. The best place to see these ungainly mammals is from the underwater floating observatory. The wide windows allow visitors to see the manatees floating in the warm spring waters like giant grey barrage balloons with fan-shaped tails. They are fed after the 1.30 p.m. program, so this is an excellent time to head for the "Fish bowl" to see them feed. The observatory also looks out on huge shoals of fish including snook, sheephead, brim, ladyfish, mullet, and catfish.

The source of the Homosassa River is the bubbling natural spring which delivers 2 million gallons of fresh spring water into the river every hour from a 35-foot deep hole. The unbelievably clear spring water is 72°F all year round, just what native manatees need to survive in the cold winter months.

Your visit is sure to be enhanced by the presence of 30 employees and rangers in green shirts, and some of the 300 volunteers who can be identified by their grey shirts. The Friends of Homosassa Springs also provide invaluable support to this lovely park which I would urge you to visit. Your first visit will certainly not be your last!

Cost

Adults $13
Children 6-12 $5

There are also group fees and annual passes available.

Opening Times

Daily throughout the year from 9 a.m. to 5.30 p.m.

Where to Eat At Homosassa Springs Wildlife State Park

Within the state park, the Wildside Café has a good choice of fast food, soft drinks and deli sandwiches. Burgers and fries, grilled chicken wraps and hot dogs are all available at reasonable prices in a very pleasant café environment at the West Entrance to the park. There are indoor and outdoor tables available and some great spots for a picnic.

Nearby Attractions

- Wild Bill's Airboats

- Don Garlit's Museum of Drag Racing and Classic Cars

- Cooter Pond Park, Inverness (see my first book *Days Out in Central Florida from The Villages*)

Favorite Days Out in Central Florida from 'The Villages' Residents

EARS – Endangered Animal Rescue Sanctuary

Recommended by Suzanne, Village of Winifred who says:

"EARS Animal Sanctuary is a rescue facility primarily for lions and tigers, but they also have bears, monkeys etc. They offer tours and give a lot of information about the animals they have rescued. A fun excursion for all ages."

Want a truly wild day out? Then make an appointment to visit the EARS Animal Rescue Sanctuary in Citra. It was one of the best animal experiences I have ever had with big cats, watching them move, purr and interact just inches away from where I stood!

The EARS Sanctuary is set on 35 acres of natural Florida countryside within an hour's drive of the Villages. Animal lovers and residents with visiting grandchildren will find a visit to EARS offers an educational and informative experience with lions, tigers, leopards, and other exotic animals which is unparalleled anywhere else. What's more, your admission enables the work at EARS to continue as a non-profit organization.

Location

EARS is north of The Villages in Citra, near Ocala.

2615 E. Hwy 318 Citra,
FL32113
Tel: (407) 647-6328

GPS Coordinates: 29.419, -82.104

www.earsinc.net

Directions

From The Villages, take Hwy 301 north to Citra.

At the traffic lights, turn right into FL318E.

The exact directions to the sanctuary will be given once you have booked your tour.

Distance from The Villages: 38 miles

What to Expect at EARS

After driving through the high security gates at EARS, leave your car in the allocated parking area and sign in. To comply with Marion County policy, visitors must become one day members of the sanctuary in order to visit. Paperwork and waivers against accident or injury must be signed before you can take a guided tour. If you have brought donations of bleach, blankets, pet food or other items, they can be handed to the volunteers at this time.

EARS was founded in 2001 by Jaye Perrett and Gail Bowen. Gail first experienced big cats during her time in Nepal and India over 20 years ago. She now lives onsite and dedicates her life 24/7 to the well-being of these beautiful creatures. CEO of EARS, and former Deputy Sheriff with the Animal Cruelty Department of Marion County, Jaye Perrett was permanently disabled during her active duty and was forced to retire from the job she loved. She has since found fulfillment by co-founding EARS and was nominated for Animal Planet's Hero of the Year Award in 2008 and 2009.

With hearts as large as the task ahead, Gail and Jaye dedicate themselves to giving exotic animals in their care a home for life, and not just a roof and food. They work incredibly hard alongside a team of 40 EARS volunteers to provide these animals with the best possible quality of life in quarters that are meticulously cleaned and disinfected daily.

Tours are led by co-founder and Vice President, Gail Bowen. Just steps away from the welcome area the cages and runs of the big cats begin. Being able to walk right up to the cage of a magnificent male lion or a pair of superb Bengal tigers is an incredible opportunity that cannot be replicated in other animal attractions and zoos. To be inches away from the yawning jaws and huge teeth of lions, tigers, cross-bred ligers and beautiful white Bengal tigers is a true privilege. Behind the individual enclosures are several huge runs, one is even having a swimming pool installed, thanks to a generous sponsor! Inside the runs there are old tree trunks and native Florida greenery for the big cats to roam, play, doze, and sleep. Generally they seemed more intent on keeping one eye on Gail, walking nonchalantly over to rub against the fence as she interacted with them and told us their history.

At the time of my visit, the sanctuary was home to over 70 animals which included 23 tigers, 3 lions, one interbred liger, several leopards, 7 Florida black bears, 2 cougars, 7 monkeys, one panther, 2 bobcats, several deer and a flock of scavenging buzzards! The sanctuary is also home to domestic cats and to several dogs that were rescued during Hurricane Katrina and were unable to be rehoused.

The animals at the sanctuary come from all sorts of backgrounds. Many of the tigers were used as cubs for photographic opportunities, but once they outgrow the cuddly stage, they are either euthanized, or the lucky ones find their way to the EARS Sanctuary. Other animals were unwanted pets, retired from animal shows, or rescued from abusive situations. The black bears often arrive as orphans;

some are returned to the wild, but for many others there is simply not the natural habitat left to provide them with a home. However, the new bear enclosures, running creek and huge run give them the best possible home in captivity.

Heat lamps are provided to keep some of the tender monkey species and other animals cozy and warm on chilly fall days and cold winter nights.

While I was there, the meat truck arrived and coolers of meat were prepared and distributed to the animals. The need for constant washing down of enclosures with bleach is evident, and every visitor is asked to bring a bottle of household bleach to help maintain the excellent standards of hygiene which the sanctuary maintains.

Gail knows the background of each animal as she introduces them, telling their sorry tales without an ounce of judgment, simply exuding love and care with her every move. Throughout the tour, volunteers can be seen stopping to interact with each animal, from cute capuchin monkeys and bush babies to communicating through voice and gesture with the large cats and bears that are keen to approach and enjoy some attention.

When I finally dragged myself away from the sanctuary, I was totally overwhelmed at having spent two hours with such beautiful creatures including lions, tigers, white Bengal tigers, leopards, panthers, bears, monkeys and many more exotic animals. What made the visit even more special was spending time with the devoted and tireless co-founder, Gail, and some of her 40 crew of volunteers. Their hard work, gentle attitude and clear love of the animals at

EARS was a true inspiration which it was a privilege to briefly come into contact with.

The private guided tours take about two hours and at the end of it you will certainly know far more about each animal than you could ever learn elsewhere. The patience and friendliness of the staff and their willingness to answer questions and volunteer information is a credit to them all. I defy anyone not to visit EARS and leave without a deep desire to help in some small way with the ongoing work, caring for these most deserving Florida residents.

Operating entirely on public donation, the admission fees provide money to keep the animals fed and housed in the very best conditions possible, with all the heating and veterinary care they need. Tours are by appointment only and groups, neighborhood socials and clubs are all very welcome.

Additional Info

Want to help?

EARS is always is need of:

- Bleach
- Blankets
- Dog and cat pet food
- Cash donations

- Building materials
- Fresh fruit and meat
- Volunteer labor
- Garden equipment

Checkout the website to see the latest wish list from the animals and their carers at EARS!

Cost

One-day membership (admission and guided walking tour)

Adults $15

Children under 10 $10

Annual and family memberships are also available.

Opening Times

Tours are by prior arrangement on any day of the week.

Where to Eat Around EARS

Midway between Ocala and Gainesville, EARS offers visitors a wide choice of places to eat out. In Citra, the Five Star Pizza or Ted's Restaurant, both on Hwy 301, have excellent reputations and are always well frequented with locals who know where to find awesome food, cheap.

Carmichael's restaurant on NE25th Ave, Ocala has good food and a growing reputation. Harry's Seafood Bar and Grill on 1st Ave, Ocala and 1st St, Gainesville never fails to satisfy. Alternatively try the new Ivy House, now opened on E. Silver Springs Blvd, Ocala on the former site of Felix's, or head for your favorite chain restaurant on SW College Rd.

Nearby Attractions

- Two Tails Ranch
- Kanapaha Gardens, Gainesville (see my first book *Days Out in Central Florida from The Villages* for details)
- Appleton Museum of Art, Ocala
- Marjorie Kinnan Rawlings Historic State Park
- Silver Springs Nature Theme Park

Favorite Days Out in Central Florida from 'The Villages' Residents

Marjorie Kinnan Rawlings Historic State Park

Recommended by Angela, Village of Tamarind Grove who says:

"I always loved the stories of Florida by Marjorie Kinnan Rawlings and when I found her home was right on the doorstep I couldn't wait to visit. I would definitely recommend the tour. I loved all the furnishings and personal touches in the homestead."

Photo: Courtesy of Florida Department of Environmental Protection

A day trip to the former home of Pulitzer prize-winning author, Marjorie Kinnan Rawlings, is an inspiration for writers, readers, and all those who appreciate Florida history. For those who are not familiar with her writing, the visit is sure to end at a second hand bookstore, searching out copies of the novels, memoirs, and cookbook of Marjorie Rawlings.

The life story of this author, who fell in love with rural Florida and made it her home, is an inspirational one. The historic homestead is simply furnished and is delightfully brought to life by interpretive guides in 1930s period dress while the grounds are a pleasure to walk around and listen to birdsong. Enjoy revisiting her home, garden, and citrus estate at this National Gold Medal Winner of Florida State Parks.

Location

The state park is located in Cross Creek, south of Gainesville on CR 325.

Marjorie Kinnan Rawlings Historic State Park
18700 S. County Road 325
Cross Creek
Florida 32640
Tel: (352) 466-3672

GPS Coordinates: 29.485, -82.161

www.floridastateparks.org/marjoriekinnanrawlings/default.cfm

Directions

From The Villages, head north on Hwy 301.

At Ocala, continue north on Hwy 301 for 23 miles. Go through Citra and after about 2 miles turn left onto CR 325. The estate is a further 3 miles on the left.

Distance from The Villages: 45 miles

What to Expect at the Marjorie Kinnan Rawlings Estate

The historic home of 1930s author, Marjorie Kinnan Rawlings, is a simple but sizeable cracker-style house with outbuildings on a 72-acre estate in the rural countryside of Florida.

As soon as you step out of your car beneath the moss-draped live oaks on the car park, the sounds of chirping insects and birdsong set the atmosphere of this lovely estate. Visitors can freely explore the grounds and peer through the windows of the various buildings for a small fee payable in the honor box on the car park.

Tours with the costumed guides are offered for a further $3 and are highly recommended. They bring together Florida history and tell the lifestory of this determined and gutsy lady who spent most of her adult life managing the estate and writing her many published works. Quotes from her books and appropriate anecdotes of her life are offered with a little light humor from the ranger and staff, who act as tour guides, making voices of the past come vividly to life for visitors.

Those wishing to join a tour should gather around the barn and sign the visitors' book in time to join the next tour of the house. Although the park is open daily, guided tours are only offered Thursday through Sunday and from October to July.

Guides are dressed in costume from the 1930s era, which for the ladies included a day dress overlaid with a pinafore, and a straw hat to keep off the sun in warm weather. Usually general introductions are made and the tale of how Rawlings came to Cross Creek is outlined before the group moves into the house itself.

The tour includes the screened porch where Rawlings' typewriter sits on the original cypress wood table, complete with palmetto palm trunk pedestal and deer-hide-covered chairs. There is no artificial air conditioning, but the raised design of the house and screened open windows and doorways create a cool and shady home in the Florida woods.

The spacious living room reveals the "dog trot" design between the open doorways. The pantry, which once stored firewood and the jealously guarded supply of alcohol that Rawlings kept during Prohibition, are part of the simply furnished room along with colorful mats, bookcases, and a fainting couch. A display cabinet of all her books includes many well-thumbed pocket-sized editions, which were printed and distributed to the forces during World War II.

Visit Rawlings' bedroom and the guest bedroom with their original furnishings, along with the dining room where she enjoyed entertaining both local friends and celebrity guests such as actor Gregory Peck and fellow author Margaret Mitchell. The rustic furniture is complemented by Rawlings' finer taste in Wedgwood china and glass.

The author used the royalties from *Jacob's Ladder* to install two bathrooms, and with her typical spirit she celebrated the installation with a party, complete with roses in the toilet and ice in the bathtub to chill the soda! The kitchen, with its original stove, is particularly interesting as this is where she enjoyed creating her recipes that led to the writing of her cookbook, *Cross Creek Cookery.* This book also reveals her talent for writing about the mundane in a totally descriptive and entertaining fashion.

The tour ends with a stroll around the fruit and vegetable patch, much as it would have been in her time. Ducks roam freely in the grounds in the company of squirrels and birds including red-headed flickers. Although the ducks might occasionally visit the nearby Orange Lake, they happily return to their pond (an old sugar cane syrup kettle) for food and safety each night.

Outbuildings include the outhouse and the tenant house where Rawlings' staff lived. On the hard standing nearby stands a sunshine yellow 1940 Oldsmobile, similar to the one she owned, rusting out its final days.

The grounds of this National Historic Landmark include shady picnic tables, a play area, and two short trails into the surrounding woodland where deer, alligators, bald eagles, bobcats, and wild turkeys make their home.

Additional Info

Those who have read Marjorie Kinnan Rawlings' books will find the Florida village lifestyle she describes, the citrus groves, neighbors and staff she features in her accounts (and was sued for on one occasion!) all come vividly to life in her well-maintained board-and-batten home.

Cost

Entrance fee to the grounds and outbuildings $3

Guided tour inside the historic home $3

Opening Times

Daily 9 a.m. to 5.30 p.m.

Tours are only offered Thursday through Sunday at 10 a.m., 11 a.m., 1 p.m., 2 p.m., 3 p.m. and 4 p.m. The house is closed during August and September for maintenance and cleaning, but the grounds remain open.

Where to Eat Around Marjorie Kinnan Rawlings State Park

The nearby Yearling Restaurant has an excellent reputation for fine food and is well worth booking a table for a special occasion.

There are several good restaurants in the downtown area of Ocala, such as Harry's Bar, or try the Ivy House on Main Street in nearby Williston and also on E. Silver Springs Blvd, Ocala.

However, the best way to savor the day in the spirit of Rawlings' outdoor life is to pick up a filled baguette from the deli counter at Publix and enjoy eating it at one of the picnic tables to the accompanying sounds of birds and insects.

Nearby Attractions

- Kanapaha Gardens (see my first book *Days Out in Central Florida from The Villages* for details)
- Silver Springs Nature Theme Park
- Endangered Animal Rescue Sanctuary, Citra
- Two Tails Ranch, Williston

Ybor City Historic Walking Tour

Recommended by Susan, Village of Springdale who says:

"This walking tour is just the best way to discover Ybor City. It's well worth the trip to enjoy a little history, shopping, and a great lunch on 7th Ave."

Ybor City is the former Cigar Capital of the World, thanks to one enterprising businessman, Vincente Martinez-Ybor. He established his cigar-making business in this historic quarter of Tampa in 1885. By 1927, Ybor City had 230 factories and was producing over 6 million cigars per year.

Favorite Days Out in Central Florida from 'The Villages' Residents

Enjoy a pleasant amble around the quiet cobbled streets on a historic walking tour, learning about the enterprising individual responsible for founding the city which still bears his name and discovering the decorative Spanish-influenced architecture in the area. The tour lasts around 1¾ hours and is led by a long-time local guide and eloquent storyteller, Lonnie Herman. You will stroll at an easy pace between shady spots and strategically placed street benches as the history of Ybor City unfolds before your eyes.

Location

Ybor City is on the northeast side of Tampa, just off I-4

The tour starts from the statue of Vincente Martinez-Ybor, at the entrance to Centro Ybor on 7th Ave and 16th St.

Tel: (813) 505-6779

GPS Coordinates: 27.968, -82.430

www.yborwalkingtours.com

Directions

From The Villages take I-75 then I-275 south towards Tampa. At I-4, turn east to exit 1 and merge onto E. 13th Ave. Turn right at N 21st St and then right into 9/8/7th Ave where there are plenty of free 2 hour parking slots.

Distance from The Villages: 82 miles

What to Expect on an Ybor City Historic Walking Tour

On arrival in Ybor City, you may be surprised at how quiet this area actually is, particularly outside the winter season. However, the area is at its liveliest at night, hence so many nightclubs along the street. Browse the excellent Visitor Center and cigar shops, or enjoy coffee or lunch at one of the cafés and restaurants. The area certainly has a lot of character with the original cobbled streets, granite curbstones, New Orleans-style architecture, fountains, and the beautiful arched entrance to Centro Ybor where the tour starts.

Meet the Cuban-hatted guide, Lonnie, who has been a local resident for over 30 years and is a walking encyclopedia of local history. He begins to tell the story of Ybor City circa 1885, with the fascinating background of Vincente Martinez-Ybor's life.

Born in Spain, Martinez-Ybor was sent to Cuba where he learned the cigar business before escaping to Key West where he built his cigar-making empire. Better transport connections, financial incentives, his good friend Gavino Gutierrez, and the chance to build his very own city eventually lured him to Tampa where he established "Mr. Ybor City." Martinez-Ybor's attempts to secure a reliable workforce led him to build workers' homes and offer ownership on very favorable terms.

As our guide built up the story of cigar-making in Ybor City, the walking tour meandered along the historic streets at an easy pace, stopping to view some of the earliest wooden homes, called "casitas". They are now part of the

National Historic Landmark District which covers 10 square blocks. On the wall of each house is the nail on which the delivery boy would have pushed the daily delivery of crusty Cuban bread!

By 1927, the cigar-making business in Ybor City was at its peak, with 230 cigar factories, and 12,000 workers producing 6 million cigars per year. However, by 1929 the Great Depression took hold; fewer cigars were sold and cigarettes became the "new" cigar. An ugly rumor (totally untrue) that cigars were hand rolled and sealed with saliva, fueled by a fear of tuberculosis, added to the marked decline in the cigar business. Finally, automation arrived and Ybor City was doomed. As factories stood empty, many of the buildings were bulldozed and the area gained a reputation as being dangerous and undesirable.

The walking tour highlights some of the key buildings still remaining on 9th Avenue, such as the mock castle exterior of the former Spanish Men's Fellowship Hall. Built in 1905, it now serves a new purpose as a nightclub. Martinez-Ybor's first factory, a huge redbrick building, is now the headquarters of the Church of Scientology, occupying the block on the Avenue Republica de Cuba between 8th and 9th Avenue. We saw the rooftop cupola, once used to look out for the ships arriving with tobacco leaves from Cuba. Once spotted, a horse and cart was dispatched post-haste to collect the tobacco from the nearby docks before it could be sold to their competitors. The tour visits the old courtyard where wives would bring a blanket and lunch for their menfolk, who would dash down the steps, eat a hasty meal and then return to their shift, for they were paid by the piece. There we learnt about the fascinating job of the lectors, who were paid by the cigar workers to read to them as they did their boring task, rolling cigars day after day.

The colonnaded building opposite the factory, built in fine Italian Renaissance style, was the Cherokee Club, the Factory Owners' Club. This became the city's first hotel, El Paso, which accommodated Presidents, State Governors and even Winston Churchill in the 1940s. Another interesting balconied building we looked inside was the elegant Don Vincente de Ybor Historic Inn, formerly a doctor's clinic and maternity home, now said to be haunted. If this tale makes you curious to know more, you may be interested in the two-hour Ybor City Ghost Tour which runs after dark, tracking the spine-chilling tales of past residents.

The historic tour visits the steps where Jose Marti made the speech which signaled the start of the revolution against the Spanish in Cuba. We also visited the pretty Parque Amigos de Jose Marti, where the Pedrosa House stood and where Marti frequently stayed under the family's protection. The park is normally kept locked, but the tour guide has a key, giving us access to the only patch of Cuban-owned soil in the USA!

The tour concludes in the Visitor Information Center in the former building of the Spanish Social Club. On the old stage, a short movie tells a quick history of Ybor City – but nothing that you won't have already heard and seen in detail from this excellent walking tour!

Additional Info

As well as the informative Historic Ybor City Walking Tour, the Ghost Tour of Ybor City may interest visitors. It takes place after dark and includes the Orpheum Theater where illicit lovers are said to haunt the basement; the King Corona premises, still the "home" of the long-deceased shopkeeper; and the Cuban Club where the ghost of a boy drowned in the swimming pool still restlessly haunts the premises.

Reservations can be made for this tour by calling (813) 386-3905. More details can be found at www.yborghosttour.com

Cost of the Ybor City Historic Walking Tour

Adults $15

Children aged 6-12 $5

Cash or check only.

Tour Times

Winter season October to April, daily at 11 a.m. and 2 p.m.

Summer season Monday-Saturday 11 a.m. and Sundays at noon. Other times by special arrangement.

Prior bookings are essential by calling Lonnie on (813) 505-6779

Where to Eat Around Ybor City

There is no shortage of excellent places to eat in Ybor City's Historic District. If you are a cigar aficionado, you will want to browse the humidors and cabinets with the many cigars on display at the turn-of-the-century premises of King Corona. Pick up some empty cigar boxes which make great gifts for under $3. Order one of their pressed hot sandwiches, pittas, or wraps, all generously packed with meat, then take an outdoor table on the sidewalk patio to enjoy people-watching along fascinating 7th Ave.

The gorgeously decorated Columbia Restaurant, on 7th Ave/22nd St, is the oldest and largest Spanish restaurant in the USA, founded in 1905. It specializes in home-cooked food and must be doing something right as it has grown from one dining room to 15, all offering a historic ambience in tasteful themed rooms.

Carmines, on 7th Ave /18th St is another popular lunch spot, famous for its deviled crabs.

Nearby Attractions

- Florida Aquarium in Tampa
- Lowry Park Zoo, Tampa
- Bok Tower Gardens (See my first book *Days Out in Central Florida from The Villages* for details)
- Sponge Divers at Tarpon Springs (See my book *Days Out Around Orlando* for details)

Two Tails Ranch

Recommended by Suzanne, Village of Winifred who says:

"Two Tails Ranch is a training, breeding and retirement facility primarily for elephants, but they have other animals as well. They give a little show of what the elephants can do and let you feed them. It is fun, educational, and very inexpensive."

If you have never seen an elephant paint, or fed carrots to one of these gentle giants, you are in for a wonderful experience at Two Tails Ranch at Williston. Founded in 1984, this private ranch facility for elephants is one-of-a-kind. It is used to board Asian and African elephants temporarily or permanently, perhaps for medical or retirement reasons, behavioral problems, during emergencies such as hurricanes, or while their home facilities are being remodeled. Having an elephant to stay does not come cheap! They eat 250-400 pounds of hay, grain, vegetables and bamboo and drink 150-300 gallons of water every day.

Seeing the contented residents at Two Tails Ranch, which is also home to a small collection of other exotic animals, is a thrilling way to appreciate and understand more about this vulnerable and endangered species.

Location

51 miles northwest of the Villages, near Williston

18655 NE 81st Street
Williston, FL32696
Tel: (352) 528-6585

GPS Coordinates: 29.460, -82.463

www.AllAboutElephants.com

Favorite Days Out in Central Florida from 'The Villages' Residents

Directions

From The Villages, take Hwy 301 north to Bellevue and join US27 north. Go through Ocala and turn right into NE 81st Street, about 3½ miles north of Williston.

Distance from The Villages: 51 miles

What to Expect at Two Tails Ranch

Visits to Two Tails Ranch must be arranged beforehand to ensure your place on one of the private guided tours. On arrival, the gate to Two Tails Ranch opens just five minutes before your scheduled tour and cars are directed to the grassy parking area. Patricia Zerbini, the CEO and co-founder of the ranch and All About Elephants Awareness Program, greets everyone and collects payment.

Just across the grassy area, the elephants can be seen contentedly grazing on piles of hay in their individual compounds. There are suitably sturdy metal posts to contain them securely. When I visited, there were four elephants in residence - Luke, Bunny, Raja and Roxy - but over the lifetime of the ranch, more than 300 elephants have passed through the gates. They are housed in huge barns heated to 62°F in the winter.

The tour begins at the seating area overlooking Luke, the 27-year old Asian male elephant. Patricia gave a short talk about elephants and then answered questions from the audience. She is the ninth generation of her family to work with exotic animals and clearly has a passion for elephants and a desire to instill awareness about the plight of elephants in their native countries. As she interacts with Luke, she looks tiny at the side of this 12,000 pound Asian elephant with his freckled trunk and perfect white tusks, which are crossed at the front.

Luke demonstrates his complete trust in Patricia by lying down at her command. He then does various poses before an artist's palette and easel are set up. He ambles over, keen to take the paintbrush from Patricia and approaches the sheet of paper on the easel. Amazingly, he judges his distance by touching the paper with the tip of his trunk and then carefully strokes the paper with the paintbrush. He steps back and is given another paintbrush loaded with another color. It is amazing to watch him paint!

The tour continues around the other animal exhibits on the ranch. This includes two spur-thighed tortoises, weighing a massive 175 pounds; Grant Zebras with their distinctive stripes which are apparently as individual as fingerprints, then around to meet Katherine the ostrich and Peppers the emu in their expansive grassy pens. After admiring Bob the cockatoo and Murphy the beautifully colored green Amazon parrot, the informative tour ends in the museum and shop. Display cases hold some interesting items relating to elephants, including a massive elephant skull, many ivory tusks, and a wonderful elephant carved in detail from a tree trunk.

The one-hour tour is a wonderful chance to see these animals close up. Guests can feed Roxy with carrots, a great opportunity to get right up close and interact with the elephant in a very unique way. The peaceful ranch environment makes a wonderful day out for all ages and your admission fee helps continue the ongoing work of this non-profit program.

Additional Info

Here are a few sobering facts about elephants:

- Elephants are in decline worldwide due to ivory poaching, hunting and loss of habitat

- Asian elephants are now an endangered species. Their numbers in the wild have dropped from 200,000 in 1900 to 35-50,000 in 2005

- African elephants are officially considered Vulnerable with numbers falling from 27 million animals in the early 19th century to less than 100,000 in 2003

- 6,000 to 12,000 elephants are killed for ivory each year in the Sudan alone

Cost

Admission/Tour: Adults $10

　　　　　　　　　　Children $5

Hand feeding an elephant $2

Cash only please.

Opening Times

Visits and tours are strictly by prior appointment and can be scheduled for any day except Thursdays. Call or email for availability.

Groups of up to 100 people can be accommodated, so consider arranging a group visit for your neighborhood social group or club.

Where to Eat Around Two Tails Ranch

The nearest town to the Two Tails Ranch is Williston where the original Ivy House Restaurant on Main Street offers lunch and dinner in the upscale restaurant. Tables are arranged throughout the rooms of this charming two-story home with a gift shop and boutique for browsing upstairs. There are also several chain fast food outlets in Williston including Subway, KFC and Hardees.

Gainesville has a good choice of places to dine, about 23 miles away. My personal favorite is Harry's Seafood Bar and Grille which serves great New Orleans style cuisine on SE 1st Street.

Nearby Attractions

- Kanapaha Gardens, Gainesville (see my first book *Days Out in Central Florida from The Villages* for details)
- EARS (Endangered Animal Rescue Sanctuary) at Citra

Wild Bill's Airboat Tours

Recommended by Donald, Village of Briar Meadow who says:

"I wanted to do something different with my grandsons, and this trip was the best! They talked about it for weeks afterwards and want to know when they can go back and hold the alligators again."

There are airboat rides, and then there's Wild Bill's Airboat Tours, emphasis on the word "Wild". This fantastic wildlife safari combines the excitement of riding on an airboat at high speed along the beautiful Withlacoochee River with wildlife spotting, bubbling springs, and the opportunity to handle a baby alligator yourself!

Featured on Fox 13 and National Geographic, this wildlife safari is a fantastic way to appreciate Florida's wildlife and scenery at its very best, and every trip is different. What's more, the return journey includes some exciting slides, 360° spins and speeds of up to 45 mph!

Location

8 miles east of Inverness on Hwy 44.

12430 E. Gulf to Lake Hwy (Hwy 44)
Inverness, FL 34450
Tel: (352) 726-6060

GPS Coordinates: 28.851, -82.225

www.wildbillsairboattour.com

Directions

From The Villages, take CR466 west over US75 to CR44.

Turn west towards Inverness and Wild Bill's is about 8 miles along, on the left.

Distance from The Villages: 17 miles.

What to Expect at Wild Bill's Airboat Tours

After signing in at the office and gift shop, visitors are directed down the trail and boardwalk onto the waiting airboat. Offering tiered bench seats, the craft can carry up to 29 passengers comfortably with great views for everyone. Don your ear protectors, and with a mighty Vroom, your adventure has begun!

Our trip with Capt. Dave took us on a journey of 9-10 miles along the broad glassy waters of the Withlacoochee River. This freshwater river is spring fed and actually runs, unusually, from south to north, ending in the Gulf of Mexico at the end of its 150-mile journey. The airboat seems to glide over the top of the water, powerfully propelled forwards by the massive fan behind the driver's seat. It seemed to ride above the floating islands of water hyacinths, reeds, and dollar weed following clear channels of water beneath the tall oaks, cypress, and palm trees.

Coots, white egrets, herons, and even a limpkin scooted out of the greenery as we zipped noisily along. However, alligators were less intimidated and we soon saw two fine specimens, 9 feet and 5 feet respectively, basking on the muddy bank. Next we saw a black and yellow-banded juvenile alligator, about three feet long, swimming on top of the shallow water. Logs were the preferred resting place of turtles and they slipped quickly into the water on our approach.

Incidentally, the river is generally only 2-3 feet deep, especially in the dry season, although it can be as deep as 25 feet in places. After the wet summer months, the river rises considerably, submerging the banks and lowlands for a time. To maintain water levels, the Wysong Lock and Dam is operated by the Southwest Florida Water Management District and this landmark was the turnaround point for our airboat safari.

The wetlands scenery kept everyone entranced as we explored narrow branches of the river before rejoining the main river. There was a continuous parade of wading birds, moorhens, ospreys, and even a bald eagle overhead. One beautiful spot we came to was the source of a natural spring. It bubbled to the surface creating a gentle boiling motion, delivering fresh spring water at a steady 72°F into a circular pool area surrounded by Cypress trees. It is a popular place for airboats and swimmers to stop and bathe during the summer. On our trip, Captain Dave cut the engines and we gently drifted in the still quietness, eventually turning full circle before heading back out to the main river.

If the outward journey is all about the wildlife, the return trip is all about having fun. Airboats are fast and incredibly versatile. They don't have brakes or reverse but they can spin through 360 degrees, do side slides, zigzag from side to side tilting and turning, and even turn around in their own wake. Accelerating quickly up to 45 mph, the ride in the open water is fast and exhilarating with spray occasionally splashing the front rows of seats, so be warned! All too soon the one hour ride comes to an end and it's time to disembark, but don't be in too much of a hurry to return to your car.

Along the main trail is the pool enclosure and home of Bubba, a 45-year-old gator that is perfect for photographing at close quarters. Right opposite the office is a shallow pool with many young alligators swimming around. After your airboat ride, staff from Wild Bill's will pick out some of the alligators, which are about 2-3 years old. They obligingly "smile" showing their teeth and posing for photographs. You can even handle one of the alligators yourself! The underbelly of the alligator is surprisingly soft while the back is supple but plated with hard bony nodules called "scutes". This particular trait of the alligator and crocodile species gives the reptiles a greater surface area for heating or cooling the blood more efficiently.

After all this excitement and interaction with wildlife, you are sure to leave Wild Bill's with a big smile on your face and plenty to talk about!

Additional Info

Reservations are recommended by calling (352) 726-6060

Cost

One hour Airboat Safari

Adults $45

Children 3-10 $35

Handling a baby alligator $3

Checkout the website which may have a discount voucher.

Nighttime airboat rides and half-day trips are also available. Group rates start from $30 per adult, so why not get a group together and have a fun trip?

Opening Times

Daily 10 a.m. to 4 p.m. all year round

Where to Eat Around Wild Bill's Airboat Tours

If you are continuing on to Inverness, there are plenty of fast food chains but few upmarket places to dine. However, if you continue past Inverness to Weeki Wachee, the Pecks Old Port Cove Restaurant on Cortez Blvd is terrific for fresh seafood. Alternatively, take a seat at the Yardarm Lounge in Homosassa which serves good food with tables overlooking Monkey Island on the Homosassa River.

If you are returning to The Villages, stop off in Wildwood at the Cotillon on Main St and sample Southern cuisine.

Nearby Attractions

- Cooter Pond Park and boardwalk, Inverness (see my first book *Days Out in Central Florida from The Villages* for details)

- Homosassa Springs Wildlife State Park

West Orange Trail

Recommended by Mary, Village of Woodbury who says:

"There are a couple of old railway trails for cycling in the area, but this is the best. We hired bikes and helmets, but you can also hire roller blades and other equipment. This is a really scenic trail which I can recommend for everyone."

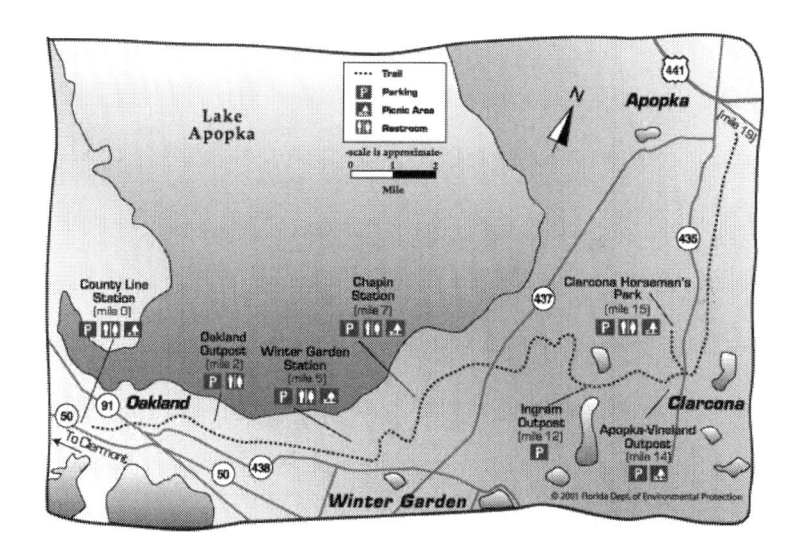

Map courtesy of Florida Department of Environmental Protection.

Discover another side to Florida with a relaxing hike or bike ride along Orlando's longest paved trail beside Lake Apopka. There are various points along the way for riders to stop, take a hike, pick up refreshments, or visit a butterfly garden. It's hard to believe that this scenic trail exists so close to metropolitan Orlando and it makes a pleasant contrast to more organized theme park activities. The trail is free of charge for walkers or those with their own equipment.

Location

The West Orange Trail runs for 22 miles through the communities of Winter Garden and Apopka. The start of the trail is just off SR50 at County Line Station on the Orange County/Lake County line. There are several other access points along the way.

Starting point:

Bikes and Blades on West Orange Trail
17914 State Road 438
Winter Garden
FL34787
Tel: (407) 654-1108 (Orange County Parks and Recreation Dept.)

County Line Station GPS Coordinates: 28.584, -81.568

Winter Garden Station GPS Coordinates: 28.551, -81.658

www.dep.state.fl.us/gwt/guide/regions/eastcentral/trails/west_orange.htm

Directions

County Line Station

From The Villages take US 27 south through Leesburg and then join Florida's Turnpike south to exit 267A.

Take the 429 Beltway north, direction Apopka. Take exit 23 and turn west on CR438, W Franklin St. After about 400 yards turn north on W Crown Point Road.

Continue north and you will soon see County Line Station Park and the start of the West Orange Trail on your left.

Distance: 49 miles

Winter Garden Station

From The Villages take US 27 south through Leesburg and then join Florida's Turnpike south to exit 272.

Turn west on FL50 for about ¾ mile and turn right into Lake Blvd and then right again on Plant Road. The Station is immediately on your right.

Distance: 40 miles

Things to Do on the West Orange Trail

Whether you hire a bicycle for the day or bring your own wheels, you are sure to have fun on this well-maintained trail through Florida's scenery and wildlife. Walkers, joggers, equestrian riders, bikers, and in-line skaters all share the trail which is also suitable for wheelchair users.

The West Orange Trail runs for 22 miles through the towns of Killarney, Oakland, and Winter Garden. It then crosses the US441 and continues through downtown Apopka to Welch Road. Most of the trail is on the former Orange Belt Railroad and it even runs down the median of Plant Street in Winter Garden where the railroad once had its tracks. After Apopka-Vineland Road it connects to a different railroad, the old Florida Midland Railroad, which takes the trail into Apopka.

This rail-trail route is smoothly paved over the entire length with no hills to worry about as it winds its way through the area. You can even take a break and explore the Butterfly Garden at the Tildenville Outpost, visit the Winter Garden Historical Museum, or spot birds and wildlife on the 2/3-mile boardwalk along the shores of Lake Apopka near Oakland.

Mile 0 -   County Line Station/Killarney Station with parking, restrooms and picnic area. Cycle hire shop

Mile 1 -   Cross the Florida Turnpike on the restored Orange Belt Railway Bridge to Oakland Nature Preserve and boardwalk to the lake

Mile 2 - Oakland Outpost with parking and restrooms

Mile 3 - Xeriscape Butterfly Garden with native plants at Tildenville Outpost

Mile 5 - Winter Garden Station with parking, restrooms and picnic area. Cycle hire shop at E. Plant St

Mile 7 - Chapin Station with parking, restrooms, sports facilities and picnic area

Mile 8 - Underpass beneath SR429

Mile 12 - Ingram Outpost with parking

Mile 13.5 - McCormick Outpost with parking

Mile 14 - Apopka-Vineland Outpost with parking, picnic area, and Korean Temple!

Mile 15 - Spur to Clarcona Horseman's Park with parking, restrooms, and picnic area. Staging area for horseback riders using the parallel trail which begins here and runs for 10 miles

Mile 19 - Cross US 441 using the new bridge to reach Apopka Station with parking, restrooms, and picnic area. Cycle hire shop at S. Forest Ave

Mile 22 - The end of the trail at Welch Road, Apopka

A future extension is planned which will eventually run along Welch Road to Wekiwa Springs State Park.

Additional Info

Bikes can be rented from Apopka Station, Winter Garden, and Killarney Station. All the bike shops are situated right on the West Orange Trail.

If you don't feel up to the 44 mile out-and-back trip, enjoy the 10 mile roundtrip from the ornate Killarney Station to Winter Garden Station, 5 miles away. This is certainly the most scenic part of the trail.

Rules of the Road

- All users should travel on the right-hand side of the trail, no more than two abreast
- Bicycles and skaters should yield to pedestrians, runners and horseback riders
- Stop and yield to traffic at all intersecting roads
- Make an audible warning when passing other users
- Pets must be on a leash

Cost

Use of the trail - Free

Bike rentals are from $6 per hour or $30 per day. Kid's bikes, trailers, tandems, and sports bikes are available in a range of sizes. Helmets are provided free of charge.

Opening Times

West Orange Trail is open daily from sunrise to sunset.

Bike Rentals Opening Hours

Bikes and Blades, SR438, Winter Garden, FL34787. Tel: (407) 654-1108

Mon-Fri 11 a.m. to 5 p.m., Weekends 7.30 a.m. to 5 p.m.

Spin City Cycles, 111 S. Forest Ave, Apopka, FL32703. Tel: (407) 886-SPIN

Tues-Fri 11 a.m. to 5 p.m., Weekends 9 a.m. to 5 p.m.

Spin City Cycles, 455 E. Plant St, Winter Garden, FL34787. Tel: (407) 877-SPIN

Tues-Fri 11 a.m. to 5 p.m., Weekends 9 a.m. to 5 p.m.

Where to Eat Around West Orange Trail

Riders should bring drinks to avoid dehydration. There are plenty of scenic picnic spots for lunch beside Lake Apopka or at one of the stations and outposts.

Downtown Winter Garden is a lovely place to have lunch. Stop off at Stromboli Inc. for a good barbecue lunch on W. Plant Street or the Plant Street Grill nearby. Scoops Old Fashioned Ice Cream Parlor is another great reason to pause for refreshments. It is adjoining the Edgewater Hotel and has a fantastic olde-worlde ambiance and a great menu of sandwiches, croissants, and sodas as well as 20 flavors of ice cream.

Apopka is slightly less chic than Winter Park but it has plenty of good places to get lunch or drinks. Bubbalou's Bodacious Bar-B-Q has won countless awards for its barbecue meats and has been run by the Meiner family since 1907. It is at the end of the trail on Rock Springs Road and is also open for breakfast for earlybirds. Further along the same road is Froggers Grill and Bar which does a tasty selection of sandwiches, burgers and subs. Go on - you can burn the calories off on the ride back!

Nearby Attractions

- Lakeridge Winery at Clermont (see my first book *Days Out in Central Florida from The Villages* for details)

- Central Florida Zoo, Sanford (see my first book *Days Out in Central Florida from The Villages* for details)

- Harry P. Leu Gardens, Orlando (see *Days Out Around Orlando* for details)

- Morse Museum and Boat Trip, Winter Park (see *Days Out Around Orlando* for details)

Forever Florida Swamp Buggy Coach Tours

Recommended by Margaret, Village of Bonita who says:

"This was the best way we found for seeing Florida's natural environment and my husband took some great photographs. The coach was comfortable and the view from so high above the ground was excellent."

Surely the best way to see Florida's wildlife is eight feet off the ground, sitting in a comfy seat with a naturalist providing a running commentary on all the animals, birds, and vegetation that come into view. This is pretty much what you get when you sign up for a two-hour fully guided coach safari with Forever Florida at the Crescent J. Ranch.

Forever Florida is part of a 4,700 acre eco ranch and conservation area which is carefully preserved as a habitat for an abundance of Florida's indigenous wildlife, including one of the highest concentrations of endangered and threatened species. This biological hotspot has nine different ecosystems which are home to alligators, bobcats, white-tail deer, wild boar, black bears, panthers, possums, armadillos, foxes, otters, skunks, snakes, turtles, and wild turkeys along with many bird species. This trip will introduce you to just some of this broad list of animals and birds who make their home in the preserve. You will certainly return home with plenty of new facts, photographs, and experiences of Florida's unique wildlife.

Location

23 miles southeast of St Cloud on Hwy 441.

4755 North Kenansville Road
St Cloud, FL 34773
Tel: (407) 957-9794

GPS Coordinates: 28.040, -81.046

www.floridaecosafaris.com/CoachSafaris/

Directions

From The Villages, take the Turnpike south to exit 244 at Kissimmee.

Take US 192 east to the flashing yellow traffic lights at Holopaw and turn south on US 441 for 7½ miles. Forever Florida at the Crescent J Ranch is on the left.

Distance from The Villages: 97 miles

What to Expect on Your Forever Florida Coach Safari

As soon as you drive through the gate to the Crescent J Ranch, you can feel the soothing effect of nature all around. Peacocks greet visitors driving up the track to the car park and butterflies flit across lily-covered ponds where dragonflies "buzz" the open water. After checking in at the Visitor Center, sit outside on one of the old rocking chairs as you wait for your group to gather.

We then climbed the metal steps and took our seats aboard the swamp buggy, high above the sandy trail with great views from the open-sided vehicle. Our guide, Nancy, was soon pointing out an alligator and a turtle before we had barely left the ranch car park! She gave us a brief history of how Dr. Broussard, a tenth generation rancher from Louisiana, bought the land in 1969 with a view to keeping it as a wildlife preserve. The family still own and live on the ranch, continuing to preserve the land under the Allen Broussard Conservancy, in memory of their son.

The swamp buggy rumbles along the sandy trail beneath shady pine trees and out into open pasture. Around 1500 acres are used for raising cattle and horses and the remainder is a wilderness preserve. Solar-powered electric fences contain the grazing area on which Charolais cattle, Cracker cattle, and horses could all be seen from our grandstand seating on wheels.

We learned that the first cattle and horses arrived in Florida with the early Spanish explorers who landed in 1521 with Ponce de Leon. After unloading their animal herd in order to begin settlement of the land, a fierce battle broke out with the Indians. The Spanish retreated, leaving their animals to their own fate and the Cracker cattle herd, with their fearsome-looking curved horns, are direct descendants of these hardy cattle. Early cow hunters would round up the cattle and drive them to market, cracking their whips to keep the animals on the move. As they approached, the townsfolk would say, "Here come the crackers", referring to the whip cracks, and the name came to mean anything native in Florida – the Cracker cattle, the Cracker wooden houses etc.

As we drove along, the coach stopped periodically for us to see alligators of all sizes from 12 inches to 12 feet in length. We saw plenty of animal tracks along the sandy trail and areas where wild boar had been scavenging for roots, leaving a destructive patch of earth. Streams and sloughs crossed the trail and cypress trees stood in ponds, their "knees" protruding from the water as part of their extensive root system. Pine flatwoods, saw palmetto, sabal palms, and plenty of wild flowers lined our path.

One stop was to see the enclosure of feral pigs which are captured and contained to prevent damage to the precious ecosystem, although plenty of their brothers and sisters still roam free.

After a further drive through the preserve we stopped and climbed down to explore the boardwalk. This well-constructed circular walkway led deep into the Cypress stand where two still lakes with brown tannic water perfectly reflected the surrounding trees. Here we learnt about how the sabal palm was used as food and shelter by the natives and the fibers were used for rope and woven for clothing – an invaluable plant for those living in the wetlands.

One Cypress tree was over 350 years old; clearly the Granddaddy of the forest. We saw spiders on perfect webs, dragonflies, butterflies, black vultures, and plenty more animal tracks as we made our way back to the coach where chilled bottles of water were handed out.

Finally, we returned to the Visitor Center having thoroughly enjoyed the two-hour tour of the "real Florida," getting up-close with nature and learning about the local wildlife.

Additional Info

From the coach tour we saw some of the other activities offered by Forever Florida. A group of horse riders passed, enjoying a horseback safari. There is also a zipline tour. All activities must be prebooked by calling (407) 957 9794

Cost

Coach Safari

Adults $32

Children aged 6-12 $28

Opening Times

Coach safaris depart twice daily at 10 a.m. and 1 p.m. and last for approximately two hours.

Where to Eat at Forever Florida

You can bring a picnic and enjoy it in the beautiful grounds beside one of the lakes at the Crescent J Ranch. However, once you push open the door of the Cypress Restaurant in the Visitor Center, you may wish you had planned to dine there. The menu includes BBQ pulled pork sandwiches, tasty hamburgers, and freshly prepared salads.

Nearby Attractions

- Kissimmee Swamp Airboat Tours • (see my book *Days Out Around Orlando* for details)

- Winter Park (see my book *Days Out Around Orlando* for details)

Favorite Days Out in Central Florida from 'The Villages' Residents

Ringling Museum of Art and Mansion

Recommended by Patricia, Village of Largo who says:

"I would like to suggest the Ringling Museum of Art as a wonderful day out. The art collection is superb and the tour of the beautiful mansion is out of this world!"

The title of the John and Mable Ringling Museum of Art is slightly misleading, as those who visit will quickly discover. There is far more to this attraction than just the world-class art collection, a legacy from the Ringlings to the state of Florida, within its purpose-built gallery. This remarkable collection includes European, American, and Asian artworks ranging from Gothic and Renaissance to contemporary paintings and sculptures.

Also within the 66-acre gardens is the stunningly beautiful Venetian-Gothic *Ca' d'Zan* mansion. This was the home of circus entrepreneur John Ringling and his wife Mable, from the mid-1920s until 1936. It is now open to the public for tours.

The 18th century Asolo Theater can be seen in the Visitors' Pavilion and is a beautiful performing arts venue. Perhaps most entertaining of all, the Circus Museum includes a huge miniature model of a typical early 20th century circus along with restored wagons, costumes, films, memorabilia, and the Ringlings' original Pullman railcar. Allow a full day for your visit, or better still, invest in a 3-day pass and spread the pleasures!

Location

Located four miles north of Sarasota near the Sarasota-Bradenton Airport

5401 Bay Shore Road
Sarasota, FL 34243
Tel: (941) 359-5700

GPS Coordinates: 27.372, -82.540

www.ringling.org

Directions

From The Villages, take US 75 south to exit 213. Then go east on University Parkway until you reach US41 and proceed straight across into the Ringling Plaza.

Distance from The Villages: 132 miles.

Things to Do at the Ringling Museum of Art

After parking in the shady car park, head for the main Visitor Center where maps, information, and tickets are available. There is also a tasteful Museum Store and the lovely Treviso Restaurant overlooking the lake and fountains.

Circus Museums

Roll up, roll up for all the fun of the circus! For most visitors, the first stop will be at the Tibbals Learning Center which houses part of the Ringling Circus Museum. After stopping to admire the beautiful circus mural and watch the short introductory film, wander around the 3,800 square foot model of a typical traveling circus in the early 20th century. The scale and logistics of having such a show on the road become apparent as you enjoy this beautifully recreated circus "village" of animals, wagons, tents, and sideshows. See the models of the rail cars that transported 1300 workers and performers, plus 800 animals, over 15,000 miles each year!

In the Golden Age of the Tented Circus (1919-1938), circuses such as Barnum and Bailey, Howard Bros, and the Ringling Brothers would cover 150 towns each season, erecting a Big Top to seat 15,000 visitors. The model is beautifully made and can be viewed from all angles to see the crowd, animals, tents, and performances along with railroad carriages and animal cages in the menagerie. The atmosphere is perfectly staged with lively circus music, lion roars, and laughter playing in the background.

Once you can tear yourself away, the second floor has a colorful collection of memorabilia, showcased miniatures, costumes, videos, and exhibits which all build up the picture of the workings of a 1920s circus. See the glorious bandwagon that was pulled through the streets of New York City by 40 black horses ahead of the traditional street parade and enjoy the interactive exhibits which are part of this display.

The neighboring Museum building is just as amazing with galleries of hand-carved animal wagons and the restored "Wisconsin" Railroad Car used by John and Mable Ringling and their friends. Built in 1905 by Pullman, the private railroad car was 79 feet long, 10 feet wide and 14 feet high and it lacked nothing. Stained glass, decorated domed ceilings, a kitchen, observation lounge, dining room, and staff quarters have all been restored to their former luxurious standard. The three staterooms had upper and lower berths which converted into sofa seating. There were washstands, toilets, and even a full-size bathtub!

During the winter, the circus originally rested at its winter quarters. From 1928 onwards, Sarasota was the chosen winter destination for the Ringling Circus, known as the Greatest Show on Earth. The mild weather allowed shows to continue throughout the winter for the first time.

Grounds and Gardens

Visitors are sure to enjoy the pleasant gardens of the Ringling Estate which include Mable's Rose Garden, the Secret Garden where John and Mable are buried, the Dwarf Garden and the Millennium Tree Trail.

The extensive grounds are laid to grass and planted with mature specimen trees including sabal palmettos, Florida's state tree, and 13 historic banyan trees with their distinctive aerial roots. There is a small lake and the property overlooks the calm Sarasota Bay towards Longboat Key. There is ample seating in wicker-style chairs for visitors to relax and enjoy the beautiful surroundings.

Ca' d'Zan Mansion

Built in Venetian Gothic style, the five-story mansion was completed in 1926 and was lavishly furnished for John and Mable Ringling. The name "Ca' d'Zan" is Venetian and means "The House of John." The pink sandstone exterior is unusually decorative and very colorful with tiled decoration, an ornate balcony, wrought iron work, and Moorish-style windows. When the mansion was built, money was clearly no object and the huge terrace overlooking Sarasota Bay is of various colorful patterned marbles enclosed by a fabulously ornate balustrade. Take a seat and enjoy the sea breeze, watching the sailing yachts, fishing boats and cruisers on the water, as John and Mable no doubt did long ago.

When you arrive at the entrance to the museum, check the tour times of the house for availability and take a self-guided tour through the lovely first floor of the house. Other optional tours and docent-led tours of the upper house and tower are also available for an additional fee and photography is allowed, without flash.

The ground floor tour begins in the solarium at specific times and then progresses through the gilt carved doors into the ballroom, foyer with its grand piano, furnished central "court" or living room, breakfast room, pantry, and kitchen. There is also a formal dining room and a quaint Tap Room, complete with bar. Many of the formal rooms have decorative coffered ceilings and there are displays of silverware, dinner services and flatware in the cupboards, just as the family would have left it.

Ringling Museum of Art

Finally, head to the pink colonnaded buildings which were completed in 1929 to house John Ringling's considerable art collection. The Renaissance-style buildings surround a sunken Italian courtyard garden complete with gushing fountains, water features, potted bougainvillea, and many statues, including a replica of Michelangelo's *David*. The original was initially installed at the entrance to the Palazzo Vecchio in Florence, Italy.

Complimentary docent-led tours of the art museum are available at certain times to help you get more from your visit to this impressive legacy of artworks, or you can stroll through the galleries reading the exhibit labels. There is also a 30-minute film of the lives of John and Mable Ringling.

The museum has some circus-themed artworks and sculptures as well as wonderful masterpieces by Rubens, van Dyck, Titian, El Greco, Gainsborough, and Velazquez. Many of these artworks were purchased by Ringling from grand European country houses which were abandoned due to expensive repairs or death taxes. These wonderful art and furniture collections had been accumulated by the aristocracy during the Grand Tours of Europe in the 18th century.

Two of the galleries in the art museum were historic salon interiors bought from the Astor mansion in New York City prior to the demolition of the house in 1926.

As you pass from room to room appreciating this remarkable legacy, you are sure to find some favorites in the paintings, silverware, statues, busts, and 20th century photographs which make up this eclectic museum.

Along with the house and gardens, this remarkable art collection was bequeathed to the state of Florida when John Ringling passed away in 1936. It is now the State Art Museum of Florida, a national treasure, giving pleasure to many thousands of visitors each year.

Cost

General Admission includes entrance to the Museum of Art, the Circus Museums, a self-guided tour of the first floor of the Ca' d'Zan Mansion, and the gardens.

Adults $25

Concessions for Seniors (65+), Students and Children

Upgrade to a 3-day Pass for an additional $10

Optional Extra Tours of Ca' d'Zan

Audio Tour of the Mansion	$5
Docent-led tour including the 2nd floor	$5
Private Places Tour including the Tower	$20

Opening Times

Daily 10 a.m. to 5 p.m. and Thursdays until 8 p.m.

Closed Thanksgiving, Christmas, and New Year's Day

Where to Eat at the Ringling Museum of Art

There are three separate dining options within the Ringling Museum of Art to suit all pockets and tastes. The Banyan Café is in the gardens close to Mable's Rose Garden and the Circus Museum. It offers snacks and drinks in a self-service environment with indoor and outdoor tables enjoying a well-designed ambience. Deli sandwiches, hot dogs, salads, cookies, and sweet treats can be enjoyed from 11 a.m. to 4 p.m. or how about trying the signature Banyan Ice Cream Sandwich?

The Store Café is part of the Museum Gift Shop and both these casual dining options are open only during Museum hours.

The classy Treviso Restaurant is one of Sarasota's finest restaurants. It is open throughout the day and into the evening, with outdoor tables enjoying views of the lake, fountains, and museum buildings. The indoor tables are spread over two floors and one wall is filled with a beautiful mural of Asolo, Italy which changes color as you dine.

Nearby Attractions

- Marie Selby Gardens
- Sarasota Jungle Gardens and Zoo
- Ybor City

- Lakeridge Winery (See my book *Days out Around Orlando* for details)

- Bok Tower Gardens (See my first book *Days Out in Central Florida from The Villages* for details)

Tarpon Springs

Recommended by Ellie, Village of Sunset Pointe who says:

"Another place I would recommend is Tarpon Springs. There is a sponge dock area with nice Greek restaurants and bakeries and a boat ride explaining how they hunt for sponges. It is a beautiful day away from The Villages."

If you fancy a taste of Greece without the long flight, pop down to Tarpon Springs, a historic Greek seaside community through and through, from the Orthodox Greek Cathedral to the Baklava bakeries and sponge diving fleet.

Stroll along Dodecanese Street in this charming Grecian-style fishing village and immerse yourself in the colorful Mediterranean culture. Browse the quaint shops decorated with strings of natural sponges or indulge in tasty pastries such as can only be found in an authentic Greek bakery. Many of these shops are owned and run by descendants of those first immigrants and retain an authentic Greek atmosphere.

Location

Tarpon Springs is 28 miles northwest of Tampa, between New Port Richey and Palm Harbor.

Tarpon Springs Visitor Center
100 Dodecanese Blvd
Tarpon Springs
FL34689
Tel: (727) 937-2952

GPS Coordinates: 28.176, -82.750

www.ctsfl.us/

Directions

From The Villages, take US301 south to Wildwood and then go west on CR44 until you get to the junction with I-75.

Go south on I-75 to junction 285 and then head west on CR52 until you reach US19.

Turn south on US19 and then right onto Business US19. If you miss the Business turn off, continue on US19 and turn west on CR582, E Tarpon Ave.

Distance from The Villages: 92 miles

Things to Do at Tarpon Springs

Tarpon Springs was settled in the late 19th century by Greek immigrants from the Dodecanese Islands. They were attracted to the area by the opportunities to dive for natural sponges, found in abundance around the shores of the Gulf of Mexico.

The Greeks had been harvesting natural sponges from the seabed around the Greek islands for centuries and the immigrants brought their skills initially to Key West. When the huge sponge beds were discovered around Tarpon Springs, local settler, John Cheyney, saw the potential and started the first sponge "hooker boat" around 1895.

By 1905 the first colony of Greek sponge divers had settled in Tarpon Springs, bringing with them their heavy diving suits and apparatus. This meant that sponges no longer had to be hooked in shallow water, but could be commercially harvested in deeper waters. Each diving suit weighed 177 pounds and had a copper helmet with an air hose, but it was still a hazardous operation.

Soon 1550 divers had settled in the area, providing a booming business for associated support industries which provided boats, diving equipment, deckhands, and staff to wash and sort the sponges for export. Tarpon Springs remained the "Sponge Capital" of America until 1946, when a toxic red tide of algae devastated the sponge beds. Almost simultaneously, synthetic sponges were introduced and the sponge-diving industry was virtually eliminated.

Although sponge diving continues on a small scale in Tarpon Springs today, the established Greek community turned to other businesses including fishing and tourism. The warehouses and Victorian mansions have been converted into shops, restaurants, B&Bs, and museums and the town continues to have the highest concentration of Greek-Americans in the U.S. within its 23,000 population.

A day trip to Tarpon Springs should include a visit to the free Spongorama Museum, a trip on a sponge-diving boat to see the divers at work, and an authentic meal in one of the Greek restaurants along the waterfront. If you're lucky you may stumble upon a raucous wedding celebration taking place in true Greek style.

The Tarpon Springs Cultural Center in the former City Hall offers a selection of historic exhibits and souvenir gifts. A walk along the waterfront will reveal the sponge tour boats and colorful fishing boats tied up near the Historic Sponge

Exchange. If you have time, squeeze in a visit to the Coral Sea Aquarium to get a glimpse of the living reef and local corals, sponges and fish in situ.

Look for the St Nicholas Greek Orthodox Cathedral, built in 1941 as a replica of St Sophia Church in Constantinople (Istanbul). It is said to be one of the most beautiful churches in the world. A peek inside reveals Byzantine architecture, 60 tons of Greek marble and a fine collection of religious artworks.

Additional Info

If you visit Tarpon Springs on the Feast of Epiphany (January 6) you can join in the oldest Greek Orthodox Festival west of Athens. The event includes the traditional diving for the Epiphany Cross, tossed into the Spring Bayou by the Archbishop of the Greek Orthodox Archdiocese of North America. Dozens of local teenage boys dive in after the Cross and the one who secures it and brings it to the surface gets a special blessing, not to mention boasting rights for a year!

Cost

Boat trips vary from $16 for a 2-hour dolphin and shelling trip (with a discount coupon from the Visitor Center) to $65 for a half-day fishing charter including lunch. Stroll along the Sponge Docks and choose a boat trip that appeals to you. The most unique are those where a diver dons the original hard hat and suit and dives for sponges from the boat.

Aquarium admission is $7 for adults with concessions for seniors and children.

Entrance to Spongorama Museum and St Nicholas Greek Orthodox Cathedral are free.

Where to Eat in Tarpon Springs

The Sponge Docks are the place to find a dozen Greek restaurants and bakeries serving meals from breakfast to dinner, accompanied by live music and dancing. It is hard to single out any particular favorite, but Hella's Bakery and Restaurant has an excellent menu from a quick gyro to a signature braised lamb or seafood dish. The bakery serves spanakopita and baklava which taste as good as they look. Mykonos is another authentic Greek restaurant, or sit outside the Parthenon which also has its own bakery, and people-watch as you dine.

Nearby Attractions

- Ybor City, Tampa
- Homosassa Springs Wildlife State Park
- Bok Tower Gardens (See my book *Days out Around Orlando* for details)

Silver Springs Nature Theme Park

Recommended by Linda, Village of Caroline who says:

"As a small girl I can remember my Grandma telling me if I ever got to Florida to be sure and go to Silver Springs and ride the glass bottom boats. There is a tour guide and each boat has different information; one is all about plant life, one is about wildlife, and one is about the movies made there. I love this funky old park!"

The wonderful water park attraction known as Silver Springs Nature Theme Park is centered on one of the many natural hot springs found in Central Florida, but this one is particularly special. Silver Springs is the largest limestone artesian spring in the world. The main spring gushes out

550 million gallons of fresh crystal clear spring water every day to become the headwaters of the Silver River which eventually runs into the St Johns River.

Glass bottom boat trips and nature tours are just one aspect of your visit to this natural theme park. There are wild animal exhibits, a petting zoo, fountain show, boardwalks, a snake show, botanical gardens, carousels and thrilling rides as well as regular concerts and a Festival of Lights at Christmas. Admission is pricey but includes many rides and attractions, although the park facilities would benefit from some updating.

Location

Silver Springs is 6 miles east of Ocala on CR40.

5656 E. Silver Springs Blvd
Silver Springs, FL34488
Tel: (352) 236-2121

GPS Coordinates: 29.219, -82.055

www.silversprings.com

Favorite Days Out in Central Florida from 'The Villages' Residents

Directions

From The Villages, take US301 north to Bellevue.

Immediately after joining US27/441 turn right onto CR25 and then CR35, Baseline Road, which will take you right into Silver Springs.

Turn right onto CR40 and the entrance into Silver Springs Nature Theme Park is on the right.

Distance: 26 miles

History of Silver Springs

Silver Springs was one of the earliest attractions in the Ocala area, with visitors arriving by steamboat and stagecoach over a hundred years ago to see this natural feature. However, the first European to witness the springs was probably Hernando de Soto, a Spanish explorer who visited the area in the early 16th century.

Hullam Jones created the first glass bottom boat in 1878 when he added a glass panel to the bottom of a dugout canoe. By the 1960s, the attraction was even more popular when visitors could visit the Ross Allen Reptile Institute and snorkel in the clear spring water.

Although many of the sideshows and attractions have come and gone, the springs continue to gush. This natural theme park offers the chance to experience Old Florida at its best.

The unspoiled Florida surroundings made Silver Springs the natural choice for the filming of six *Tarzan* movies starring Johnny Weissmuller. Monkeys brought in for the filming were later released and their offspring now inhabit the area. Cute moms with babies on their backs can be seen on the riverbank as tour boats pass by. Other films shot on location at Silver Springs include *The Creature from the Black Lagoon,* filmed in the 1950s, along with the 1960s TV series *Sea Hunt* starring Lloyd Bridges. The cabin that served as his dressing room can still be seen on the river bank.

Things to Do at Silver Springs

Today the springs are part of the 350-acre nature theme park of Silver Springs, which is listed on the National Register of Historic Places. The spring waters bubble up at a constant 72°F in the natural basin which is 300 feet wide and 80 feet deep, accommodating the largest artesian spring in the world.

Glass bottom boats are a great way to see what's happening below the surface of the moving waters. Trips are on pontoon boats with open sides and glass bottoms for viewing the underwater world. Tours include an experienced narrator who explains some of the facts about the springs and the aquatic wildlife. It is so exciting to see fish of all sizes swimming below the boat along with turtles, crawfish, snails, clams, and other creatures.

The boats also give a good view of the cracks in the limestone riverbed which allow many more springs to add to the spring run.

On the boat trips, alligators can be seen dozing on the river banks as visitors walk on the paths nearby, oblivious to their presence. There are many different species of turtles swimming and sunning themselves on logs along the edge of the Silver River along with herons and other wading birds.

Fort King River Cruise takes you on a journey back through 10,000 years of history. Visitors will see an archaeological dig site, a Seminole Indian village, an 1830s stockade, the old train depot which once brought visitors flocking to Silver Springs, and an authentic Cracker homestead on the property.

The Big Gator Lagoon is home to some of Florida's largest alligators, reaching up to 13 feet in length. Other exhibits include White Alligators, some of the rarest reptiles on earth. They are nicknamed "Swamp Ghosts" and you will understand why when you see them.

See cougars at the Panther Prowl exhibit and get up-close with snakes, spiders and other small Florida creatures at Ross Allen Island. The World of Bears is one of the largest exhibits of its kind in the world. There is also a petting zoo where friendly farm animals love being fed and stroked.

Thrilling rides in the park include the 80-foot high Lighthouse Ride which gives great views of the park from the gondolas. Watch the Free Flight show of raptors, owls,

Amazonian parrots and cute ducks. See the alligators and crocodiles being fed by keepers, and learn about venomous snakes at the Snake Show. Walk the boardwalks through the pretty floral garden or rest your feet on a tram ride along the Wilderness Trail, towed behind a Wrangler Jeep.

Silver Springs is certainly a full day out with plenty of activities suitable for all ages, from tots to grandparents. The park also puts on a program of outdoor concerts, car shows and special events throughout the year and many well-known performers including Crystal Gale, Roy Clark, Tanya Tucker and Clint Black have performed here.

Cost

One Day Admission

Adults $34.99

Children 3-10 $26.99

There are a variety of Annual Passes from $51.99 offering admission and parking for 12 months, including access to special events and limited access to daytime or nighttime concerts.

Opening Times

Opening times vary with seasons and special events. See website or phone for details.

Generally the park is closed Mondays and Tuesdays in the winter season and only opens at weekends in summer.

Open 10 a.m. to 5 p.m. on certain days with later hours for special events such as concerts, Halloween and the December Festival of Lights.

Where to Eat at Silver Springs

You certainly won't go hungry at Silver Springs with snack bars and ice cream shops around the park.

For lunch choose from the Springs Pizzeria, the Springside Café, the Deli, or the Billy Bowlegs Bar and Grill which is open during special events. The café serves burgers, hot dogs, a fish basket, and other American cuisine in a pleasant atmosphere.

Nearby Attractions

- Don Garlits Museum of Drag Racing and Classic Cars
- Endangered Animal Rescue Sanctuary (EARS)
- Marjorie Rawlings Historic State Park

- Wild Bill's Airboat Tours

- Cooter Pond Park, Inverness (See my first book *Days Out in Central Florida from The Villages* for details)

St Augustine

Recommended by Donna, Village of Tall Trees who says:

"Whenever we have houseguests we always take them to St Augustine. There is so much to do there – the little train tour, the fort, museums, and the historic district. Everyone we take loves the old shops and Spanish buildings."

Many people complain that Florida has no real history. It's true, it does not have much compared to Europe, but the history it does have is very impressive. For example, did you know that America's oldest continuously occupied settlement is St Augustine in Florida?

This lovely city has a relaxed ambience and is full of history and old world charm. The narrow streets, Spanish-style architecture, Bridge of Lions and quaint shops along St George Street make this a delightful place to spend a day. The historic quarter includes America's Oldest Wooden Schoolhouse, colonial dwellings and the old City Gates.

Location

53 miles north of Daytona Beach, on Florida's First Coast.

Visitor Information Center
W. Castillo Drive/Cordova St
St Augustine FL32084
Tel: (904) 484-5160

GPS Coordinates: 29.902, -81.315

http://www.ci.st-augustine.fl.us/

Directions

Take CR466 east to 27/441 then, almost immediately, go north on CR25.

On reaching CR40, turn east until the junction with CR 11.

Turn north here and join US1. Continue heading north to reach St Augustine.

Alternatively, follow the directions to Daytona Beach and then take either US1 or I-95 north to St Augustine.

Distance from The Villages: 109 miles

Things to Do in St Augustine

St Augustine is a truly historic city with many attractions, a fortress, museums, historic houses, and beautiful architecture in the heart of the city.

St Augustine was founded in 1565 by Pedro Menendez de Aviles on the feast day of St Augustine, and this is how the city got its name. In 1702, it burnt down and was rebuilt in the shadow of the huge Castillo de San Marcus. Many of these 300-year-old buildings can still be seen today, lining the pretty, narrow streets of the historic district.

In 1883, railroad magnate Henry Flagler visited St Augustine on his honeymoon. He was so impressed with the area that he built the grand Ponce de Leon Hotel in

1888, now the centerpiece of Flagler College. Wealthy visitors began to follow his example, traveling by train to Florida's East Coast and soon St Augustine was a popular tourist destination, as it continues to be today.

Visitors will find St Augustine is a charming and unique city. It is quite compact and easy to walk around with plenty of lovely pavement cafés and high-end restaurants. Trolley tours are a great way to learn about the main historic sites with an informative guide. Stroll to the old fort, the Castillo de San Marcos, which overlooks the Intracoastal Waterway spanned by the Bridge of Lions. The fort is a National Monument, managed by the National Park Service. Visitors can walk the casements, watch videos, view re-enactments and weapons demonstrations, or take an interpretive walk with a ranger. Take a ghost tour of the city or visit the incredible Ripley's Believe It or Not! attraction nearby, which is interesting for all ages.

Enter the Old City Gate and wander along the cobblestone streets to the Plaza de la Constitution. Explore the Colonial Spanish Quarter nearby with its charming higgledy-piggledy buildings, including America's oldest wooden schoolhouse. A massive chain encircles this cypress and red cedar building and anchors it to the ground during high winds! This traffic-free area has a collection of historic buildings and small shops selling ice cream, chocolates, gifts, and antiques. Some of the interesting attractions include the Spanish Quarter Museum which has seven reconstructed buildings with costumed interpreters demonstrating crafts and skills from the mid-18th century.

In contrast, King Street is the heart of the more modern city. Lined with beautiful Spanish-influenced architecture, it is very pleasant to stroll along and admire the buildings such as Government House with its Spanish-style loggias and Zorayda Castle with its Arabic motifs, a replica of the fabulous Alhambra Palace in Granada, Spain. Further along King Street, the Hispanic-Moorish building that was once the Alcazar Hotel now houses the impressive Tiffany glass and antiques of the Lightner Museum collection.

One-hour tours of the Ponce de Leon Hall are well worth taking to see inside this lovely Spanish Renaissance-style building. It was constructed in 1888 as the Ponce de Leon Hotel and is now a National Historic Landmark, part of the Flagler College campus. It was designed by architects John Carrere and Thomas Hastings, who went on to build New York Public Library and the House and Senate buildings in Washington D.C. It features Tiffany designed mosaics, stained glass windows, and beautiful murals by George Willoughby Maynard and Virgilio Tojetti. You can just imagine that it was quite a wonderful place to stay in its time and was one of the first hotels in the country to have electricity. The grounds are also very pleasant to stroll around.

There are several beaches around St Augustine including the white sands of Anastasia Island, just five minutes from downtown. It has a pier, playground, pavilion, cafés, and shops. Crescent Beach is also on Anastasia Island, a wildlife refuge with a natural setting that is popular for beachcombing. Vilano Beach is said to be the area's best kept secret with waterfront restaurants, a fishing pier, parasailing, and SeaDoo rentals.

Cost

St Augustine as a city is free to visit but various attractions charge admission/tour fees.

Old Town Trolley Tours

Adults $23.69

Children 6-12 $10.30

Old Fort

Adults $7 (7-day access)

Children under 15 Free when accompanied by an adult

Ponce de Leon Hotel/Flagler College Tours

Adults $10

Children under 12 Free

Colonial Spanish Quarter Historic District

General admission to the street – Free

Ripley's Believe It or Not!

Adults $14.99

Children 6-11 $7.99

Seniors $12.26

Lightner Museum

Adults $10

Teens 12-18 $5

Under 12   Free

Opening Times

See individual attractions for opening times

Where to Eat in St Augustine

Just along St George St there are a number of sidewalk cafés offering everything from coffee and cakes to sandwiches and light lunches. For a more substantial meal in nice surroundings, try the Aviles Restaurant in the Hilton

Hotel on Avenida Menendez. It has an international menu including some Spanish specialties as a nod to this Spanish-influenced city.

Nearby Attractions

- Anastasia Island
- Vilano Beach
- De Leon Springs State Park

De Leon Springs State Park

Recommended by Anne, Village of Charlotte who says:

"I thought De Leon Springs State Park would make a great day trip for anyone, especially if you have grandchildren visiting. There's hiking, picnic areas, eco-boat rides, and a wonderful lake for swimming year round. We recommend this park to all our friends and everyone raves about it."

The central attraction at De Leon Springs is the warm natural spring, pouring forth clear, warm water at a rate of 19 million gallons per day. Swimming, diving, kayaking, boating, hiking, fishing, and more can all be enjoyed at this lovely state park. Plan to come for the day and bring the grandchildren – there is plenty to see and do!

Although Florida has a relatively short history, there is evidence of human settlement beside De Leon Springs for over 6,000 years. Looking at the tall palms, prickly shrubs, and mass of dense roots in the swampy wetland, you can appreciate the struggle that the native Indians, European settlers, and their slaves had in order to tame the hostile jungle environment. The Visitor Centre at De Leon Springs State Park tells the story with excellent exhibits, old photographs, and quotes from the early settlers far better than I can possibly describe, so don't miss out on a visit to this informative museum/information center overlooking the bubbling springs.

Location

De Leon Springs State Park is 6 miles north of DeLand, off US17.

601 Ponce De Leon Blvd
De Leon Springs, FL32130
Tel: (386) 985-4212

GPS Coordinates: 29.130, -81.360

www.floridastateparks.org/deleonsprings

Directions from The Villages

From The Villages, take US301 north to Bellevue, then continue north on Hwy 35 to Hwy 40 at Silver Springs.

Go east on Hwy 40 until you reach US17, turn south to De Leon. From there, follow the signs, turning right on Lake Winona Road. After about a mile you will see the entrance to the state park on the left.

Alternatively, a more scenic route, is to take the CR466 to the 27/441. Turn north and then, almost immediately, go north on CR25 to Weirsdale. Turn east on the CR42 and then join Hwy 44 to DeLand.

In DeLand follow signs for US17 north and continue along US17 until you reach De Leon. The entrance to the park is on the left via Lake Winona Road

Distance from The Villages: 68 miles

Things to Do at De Leon Springs State Park

Just driving to De Leon Springs State Park is a wonderful trip through some of Florida's most natural acreage. After admittance at the gate, there is ample car parking around the state park, all well laid out beneath the spreading branches of ancient oaks, cypress, and palm trees. After walking past dozens of picnic tables on the short grass, the first sight to greet visitors is the large circular swimming pool that nature, with a little help from man, has created.

The pool is about 60 feet across and ranges from 2-30 feet in depth. The water is incredibly clear and towards the center of the pool it gently simmers, indicating where the springs, under great force, bubble up from the giant aquifer on which Florida is built.

There is no shortage of entry points to the swimming area for would-be swimmers: steps, ladders, diving stations and a gentle ramp are spaced at intervals around the pool, which incidentally remains at 72°F all year round. Most visitors come here to walk the trails, enjoy a picnic in this peaceful natural park, or swim, snorkel, and dive in the crystal clear waters under the watchful eye of a lifeguard in the summer season. Fishing can be enjoyed from the shore or fishing pier, and judging by the shoals of fish I saw hanging out under the walkway, it should be fairly easy to hook a good catch.

The giant swimming pool empties in a gushing cascade over natural rocks into the main flow which becomes the St Johns River. This is where kayaks and paddleboats are available for hire, to explore some of the 18,000 acres of lakes, creeks, and marshes. This is also where the boat trips on the M/V Acuera pontoon boat start.

The 50-minute eco/history tours take visitors on a peaceful journey through the Lake Woodruff National Wildlife Refuge. Capt. Frank is skilled in the art of spotting turtles, manatees, alligators, otters, herons, egrets, coots, and ospreys that all call this area "home" and he provides an informative narrative during the tour.

Those wanting some more strenuous exercise can hike the ½ mile paved nature trail. Take the detour along the short boardwalk to see "Old Methuselah", a huge bald cypress tree that is over 500 years old. Returning to the main trail, head out beneath the shady live oaks on the footpath, which is liberally covered in pine needles and pine cones, to Monkey Island.

There is a much longer and more arduous 4.2 mile Wild Persimmon Trail Loop through the surrounding lowlands. The area is full of red maples, sweet gums, magnolias with their fragrant white blooms in early summer, cabbage palms, water hickories, and cypress trees with their "knees" clearly visible above the still waters. Azaleas were also planted here between the 1930s and the 1960s, adding a splash of showy color in early spring.

Facing the Visitor Center and the spotless restrooms is the Old Spanish Sugar Mill Restaurant. It is in the wooden mill-style building which still has the original huge waterwheel on the side.

History of De Leon Springs

The presence of human settlement in the De Leon Springs area was confirmed by the discovery several large mounds of discarded snail shells (called middens) and earthen mounds. These were used by early man as trash heaps, burial places, and for ceremonies. The mound found at De Leon Springs is about 6,000 years old and it extends under the Visitor Center, north of the pool area.

In 1985, a canoe was removed from the springs and was carbon dated to about 3100 BC. Five years later an even older canoe was discovered, dating back to 4050 BC. These are the oldest canoes ever found in the western hemisphere.

Little would have changed in this area until the 19th century when Major Joseph Woodruff bought 2020 acres around the springs and created Spring Garden Plantation. Using about 250 African slaves, without whom the area never would have been cleared for agriculture, the plantation produced cotton, corn, rice, and sugar cane.

De Leon Springs had a famous visitor in 1831, the naturalist John James Audubon. The detailed account of his visit is recorded in the Visitor Center, along with historic information about local Civil War activity and the Seminole Wars.

In the 1880s, the railroad arrived and De Leon Springs became a fashionable resort. It was promoted as the "Fountain of Youth" with "Healing Waters". By the 1920s, a hotel had been built with 14 rooms overlooking the swimming pool/springs. Known as the Ponce De Leon Springs Inn, it had a private dance floor, casino, and restaurant. In 1933, a $1million renovation project added beautiful gardens, jungle cruises, a cocktail lounge, gift house, and tram tours through the beautiful grounds. A water circus show included an elephant water skiing! Sadly, the hotel was not maintained and was eventually demolished in the 1950s.

Threatened with development in 1980, the area was purchased by Volusia County, aided by the state, and De Leon Springs State Park was opened in 1982.

Cost

Entrance per car $6

Boat trips $14 per person over the age of 4

Opening Times

8 a.m. to sunset daily

Where to Eat Around De Leon Springs State Park

This lovely attraction is perfect for a picnic, but if you want to buy snacks there are concession stands around the swimming pool area along with the Old Spanish Sugar Mill Grill and Griddlehouse. The sensibly-priced menu includes salads, hot sandwiches such as BLT or the popular All You Can Eat Pancakes for $4.95 with honey, syrup or molasses. Other more decadent pancake toppings are available for a small extra charge.

Nearby Attractions

- The city of DeLand with its elegant college buildings, restored theater, and City Hall

- Blue Spring State Park (see my first book *Days Out in Central Florida from The Villages* for details)

- New Smyrna Beach

Daytona Beach

Recommended by Judith, Village of Buttonwood who says:

"I prefer Daytona Beach to Cocoa or New Smyrna Beach as there is so much to do there. We take a cooler and beach chairs and enjoy a long walk on the beach then relax and watch the surfers."

Daytona Beach is a 23-mile stretch of gorgeous golden sand running down the Atlantic coast of Florida, south of St Augustine, and just north of New Smyrna Beach. It makes a great day out for those wanting to spend the day on the beach as you can drive right onto the sand in the vehicle-accessible areas. There is a pleasant mall for shopping, restaurants, and several attractions nearby to fill the day.

The city of Daytona Beach is a sizeable community with a marina, the Volusia Mall, and Daytona International Speedway. There is a good range of waterfront dining and all the usual small businesses you will find in any Florida community from tire shops to real estate agencies, banks, liquor stores, fast food restaurants, Starbucks, Wal-Mart, Sams Club and Walgreens. If you need anything, you will find it in Daytona Beach!

Location

75 miles northeast of the Villages between New Smyrna Beach and St Augustine.

GPS Coordinates: 29.225, -81.024

www.daytonabeach.com

Directions

Take the CR466 to the 27/441. Turn north and then, almost immediately, go north on CR25 to Weirsdale.

Turn east on the CR42 and then join Hwy 44 to DeLand.

In DeLand follow signs for US17 north and then go east on E International Drive (CR92) to Daytona Beach.

Distance from the Villages: 75 miles

Things to Do at Daytona Beach

Daytona Beach has firmly packed sand and rolling waves making it ideal for surfing, sunbathing, kite-surfing, or long walks in the constant breeze. There are trained lifeguards in the most popular areas of the beach with warning flags indicating local conditions. They also post information on the tide and temperatures. Even on the hottest day the beach is bearable if you have some shade from an umbrella and an onshore wind. A great place for youngsters to cool off is in the Sunsplash Park which has jet fountains and an undercover playground to give children a place to play in the shade.

The beach is overlooked by hotels and high-rise apartment buildings, many of which are shuttered against hurricanes as their owners visit for just a few weeks each year. The more popular buildings tend to be timeshare-owned with beautiful swimming pools and tiki bars overlooking the beach. There are some amusement parks and fun fair rides along Daytona Beach, but as you travel further south the beach becomes quieter and is overlooked by private beach houses of all sizes and ages. The best thing about Daytona Beach is that for around $6 you can drive your car onto the beach and park for the day. Vans patrol up and down selling drinks and snacks and there are regular beach patrols.

There are plenty of things to do around Daytona Beach apart from the beach and shops. Take a relaxing trip on the Halifax River to see the dolphins, birds, and wildlife. In the winter, the St John's River is where many manatees gather to feed. Alternatively, take the Daytona Trolley Bus Tour around the sights or enjoy a tour in one of the amphibious vehicles that start on the highway and then plunge into the river. The Museum of Photography and the Ormond Memorial Art Museum are also worth paying a visit.

One of the most modern entertainment areas is at the end of Main Street and is known as the Ocean Walk Village. The complex has several upmarket hotels and a theater, shops, amusements, oceanfront dining, bars, and restaurants. Right across the street from Ocean Walk Village is the Convention Center and the Daytona Lagoon Waterpark and Arcade. Nearby is a children's playground, fun center, boardwalk, and the pier.

It was the miles of firm sand on Daytona Beach that gave birth to it becoming the home of supercharged speed. The first Daytona Speedway races ran for almost 50 years on an unofficial racing circuit that included the beach and part of the A1A Highway, which runs parallel. Finally, the racing was placed on a more permanent footing when the Daytona International Speedway was built in 1959 on what became known as International Speedway Drive. The stadium has since become a landmark of the area. The track is 2½ miles long and the building of the improved circuit coincided with faster and more reliable racing cars, so the main race was increased from 200 to 500 miles in length.

When races are not in progress, visitors can take a guided tour of the huge stadium on the 480-acre site. Guides take you behind the scenes to see what is involved in making NASCAR events run smoothly. Visitors get to see the Drivers' Meeting Room, tour the NASCAR Spring Cup

Series garages, view the Victory Lane, and take a peek inside the press box, seven floors above the track itself.

Additional Info

Driving is generally allowed on Daytona Beach in the vehicle-accessible areas from one hour after sunrise to one hour before sunset. However, in the turtle nesting season (May1 to Oct 31), driving hours are strictly between 8 a.m. and 7 p.m. Drivers must stick to the driving lanes, park in the designated areas, and maintain the 10mph speed limit.

Dogs are not permitted on Daytona Beach.

Cost

The beach is free for pedestrians and cyclists, but a $6 charge is made per vehicle.

Opening Times

The beach is open 24/7 but cars are only allowed onto the beach at certain times. See Additional Info for exact details.

Where to Eat Around Daytona Beach

A particular favorite restaurant of mine is the Hyde Park Steakhouse Restaurant in the Hilton Hotel where you can get great deals on cocktails from 5pm with small plates of lite bites and superb steaks with excellent side dishes. It is an upmarket restaurant but the deals and early bird specials make it a great value place to dine with topnotch waiter service.

For somewhere relaxed and affordable, try Caribbean Jack's Restaurant and Beach Bar on Ballough Road, which has an excellent menu and plenty of tables overlooking the Intracoastal Waterway. Live music ensures it stays busy and lively at night, but lunchtimes are quieter and very pleasant.

Nearby Attractions

- Ponce Inlet Lighthouse
- DeBary Hall at Deltona (see my book *Days Out in Central Florida from The Villages* for details)
- De Leon Springs State Park
- Blue Springs State Park (see my book *Days Out in Central Florida from The Villages* for details)
- St. Augustine

Don Garlits Museum of Drag Racing and Classic Cars

Recommended by Tom, Village of Hemingway who says:

"We are so fortunate to have this world class museum of drag racing on our doorstep. It's not just for racing fans. There is an excellent classic car museum too."

Few people seem to know that The Villages is just around the corner from one of the most comprehensive collections of specialized vehicles in the world. Don Garlits Museum of Drag Racing and Classic Cars is not just a collection of old cars, it is the lifestory of a legend – Big Daddy. The succession of his home-built "Swamp Rat" dragsters tells the incredible story in its own inimitable fashion as you walk around more than 200 vehicles, driven, built or in some way associated with Don Garlits, the #1 Drag Racer who dominated the sport from the 1950s until his retirement in 1992.

On the same site as the Drag Car Museum, in an adjacent building, is the Museum of Classic Cars, another comprehensive collection of around 80 antique and classic cars from the early 1900s to a beautiful 2003 Corvette Convertible Anniversary model. This is a day out even for those who are not big fans of car museums. After all, as Roadside America says, "Dragsters aren't really cars – they're horizontal missiles with wheels!"

Location

8 miles west of Summerfield, on CR 484

13700 SW 16th Ave
Ocala, FL 34473
Tel: (352) 245-8661

GPS Coordinates: 29.024, -82.153

www.garlits.com

Directions

From The Villages, drive west on CR 466. Where the road turns north (next to I-75), continue on CR 475 until the flashing red lights.

Turn left onto CR 475A and continue until you reach Don Garlits Museum on your left, just before the junction with CR 484.

Distance from The Villages: 14 miles

What to Expect at Don Garlits Museum of Drag Racing and Classic Cars

Don Garlits Museum of Drag Racing and Classic Cars is very easy to find, within sight of Exit 341 on I-75. You know when you've arrived as there is a huge A-7 US Navy jet on the parking lot. This commemorates when he beat one in a drag race on the flight deck of an aircraft carrier, as a stunt to persuade draft-eligible kids to join the Navy during the Vietnam War.

The entrance to the museum is inside the well-stocked gift shop. Step through the doors into the huge 50,000 square-foot hangar-type space which is filled with aisles of gleaming dragsters spanning over seven decades of drag racing history. Each immaculate vehicle has an information board with full spec. and history, which builds up an incredible story of the achievements of "Big Daddy."

Don Garlits dominated drag racing as the indisputable champion from his first win of a National Hot Rod Association event in 1955. He went on to earn every major dragging honor at least once, winning 50 consecutive matches and almost 100 major events. In his iconic "Swamp Rat" he owned the quarter-mile world speed record, reaching 252.7 mph in 5.6 seconds. In 1988, Garlits qualified for the 200 mph Club in his Swamp Rat 33 – he actually went down the track at 215.093 mph and returned at 220.802 mph. In a period of just two years, the "Swamp Rat," as Don Garlits was nicknamed, won 24 out of 30 national events and collected prize money of over $606,000.

The Museum of Drag Racing vividly tells the story of all these incredible achievements, and shares some of the horrific moments of his racing history through videos, photographs, and information boards. Altogether there are over 200 quarter-milers on display, including restored fuel dragsters, stock cars, funny cars, exhibition cars, and even the first motorcycle to break the 200 mph barrier. Huge display cases line the walls filled with gleaming trophies, cups, and medals which tell the story of this prolific winner. There is also a mesmerizing array of personal memorabilia, photographs, advertising boards, clothing, and yet more photographs spanning the career of a racing legend from the 50s to the 90s.

Once you have OD'd on dragsters, walk down to the second building which continues the tour with an equally impressive collection of more than 80 antique and classic cars. Beautifully restored and immaculately polished, the rows of cars include a 1904 Orient Buckboard (open top motoring at its best!), 1909 Buick Model 10, 1928 Ford Roadster Pickup, 1929 Ford Model A Tudor, and a 1932 Ford V8 Roadster. Station wagons, sedans, and coupes include Corvairs from the 1960s, a Dodge Charger, and a cross section of Chryslers, Chevys, and trucks are on show, all built to run in the days when gas was just 19 cents a gallon!

The building also has more general motoring memorabilia and the layout of Don's original garage from 1956 in Tampa. Frequent mention is made of his wife, Pat, and his brother Ed, making this a very heartwarming family saga of hard-earned success. What a man! What a life story! And what a Museum! This incredible collection of cars will blow you away with its phenomenal stories and exhibits behind the "King of Drag Racing." Don Garlits continues to spend time on site, and if you're really lucky you may get to spot him and shake his hand! Otherwise, Francine on the admissions desk is more than willing to answer most questions knowledgeably and with a ready smile.

Additional Info

The Museum Gift Shop is the perfect place to find gifts for motorheads and racing fans. Autographed memorabilia includes all sorts of bits and pieces from when "Big Daddy" clears out his garage. How about an autographed chrome-plated cylinder cap, or a signed baggie of used spark plugs? The beautiful book *Don Garlits and His Cars* is the comprehensive record of each of Don's racing cars and Swamp Rats, written by Don himself, and makes a wonderful souvenir of your visit.

Cost

Adults $15

Seniors 60+ $13

Opening Times

Open daily 9 a.m. to 5 p.m. except Christmas

Where to Eat Around Don Garlits Museum

Just around the corner from Don Garlits Museum is Cracker Barrel which serves home cooking in an antique store setting. Heading back to the Villages on CR 42, drop into Beef O'Brady's Sports Pub at Mulberry Grove for lunch. It has a menu of wings, burgers, and fried shrimp in an informal atmosphere.

For more upmarket fare in a very pleasant setting, the Legacy Restaurant at Nancy Lopez Country Club does a range of steaks, fish, and seafood with prices a little on the high side. Better value is offered at the adjoining Oasis Bar and Grill overlooking the swimming pool with a choice of typical "pub" fare for under $10.

Nearby Attractions

- Cooter Pond Park, Inverness (see my first book *Days Out in Central Florida from The Villages* for details)

- Wild Bill's Airboat Tours

- Silver Springs Nature Theme Park

- EARS (Endangered Animal Rescue Sanctuary), Citra

Gillian Birch

OVER TO YOU

If you enjoyed these Favorite Days Out in Central Florida from 'The Villages' Residents, please **POST A REVIEW** on Amazon.com, or consider contributing your ideas to the next book:

More Days Out in Central Florida from 'The Villages'

If you would like to suggest a favorite day out which has not yet been covered, I would love to hear from you. The most suitable destinations will be visited and included in the next book. They will include the proposer's name (or pseudonym) and home Village, along with a short comment on what makes your suggested destination a great day out from 'The Villages'.

Please email details of your favorite day out in Central Florida to me at yourtravelgirl@gmail.com

Please include:

- Your name
- Your home Village
- Your contact details
- A sentence or two on why this is your favorite day out from the Villages

If your suggestion is chosen to be included in the next book, you will get to see your name in print and a complimentary copy of the book, signed by the author, will be sent to you.

Gillian Birch

COMING SOON

Look out for more books by Gillian Birch in this series:

- Days Out in Central Florida from 'The Villages'
- Days Out Around Orlando
- 20 Best Florida Beaches and Coastal Cities
- Days Out in Central Florida with Children
- Favorite Days Out in Central Florida from 'The Villages' Residents
- More Days Out in Central Florida from 'The Villages'
- Historic Homes in Florida
- Beautiful Gardens in Florida

These will be available in paperback from Amazon.com, Barnes & Noble and local bookstores, and will also be available as downloadable ebooks.

You can also keep up with future publications at: www.gillianbirch.com

Gillian Birch is also the Florida Editor of BellaOnline, an online magazine for women. Enjoy her weekly articles at http://www.bellaonline.com/site/florida featuring places to visit and things to do in Florida. There are additional links to join in the conversation on the BellaOnline Florida Forum, or subscribe to her free Florida newsletter.

Gillian Birch

ABOUT THE AUTHOR

Gillian Birch is a freelance travel writer and published author. As the wife of a Master Mariner, she has traveled extensively and lived in some exotic locations all over the world, including Europe, the Far East, the Republic of Panama, and of course 'The Villages'. Her love of writing led her to keep detailed journals which are a valuable source of eye-witness information for her many published magazine articles and destination reviews.

Describing herself as having "endless itchy feet and an insatiable wanderlust," she continues to explore Florida and further afield with her husband, writing about her experiences with wonderful clarity and attention to detail.

Gillian has a Diploma from the British College of Journalism and is proud to be a member of the International Travel Writers' Alliance and the Florida Writers' Association. Learn more about her writing as YourTravelGirl at www.gillianbirch.com

Made in the USA
Columbia, SC
09 December 2018